The "Teaching of English" Series

General Editor—Sir Henry Newbolt

ESSAYS AND ESSAYISTS

No. 26

OLIVER GOLDSMITH

From a pen-drawing by
E. Heber Thompson

❧ ESSAYS AND ❧ ESSAYISTS

Compiled and Edited
by
HENRY NEWBOLT

❧

THOMAS NELSON & SONS, LTD.
LONDON AND EDINBURGH

First published in this Series May 1925

PRINTED IN GREAT BRITAIN AT
THE PRESS OF THE PUBLISHERS

CONTENTS

INTRODUCTION

It may seem an inconsistency to begin a volume of English Essays with the work of a man who was not English at all. But there is no way of avoiding this if I am to carry out my intention ; which is to provide the reader with material for the study of a particular form of literature, undoubtedly derived from a single French original. It is a form used by our own people for more than three hundred years in a fashion of their own and with a distinctive success : but the qualities of the ancestor are still strongly marked in his posterity, and they could not, if they would, deny their descent. As a matter of fact they are in general both conscious and proud of it, as will appear presently.

It is well known that the various forms of literature are for the most part very ancient. History, Oratory, Dialogue, Drama, Epic, Idyll, Lyric, and Epigram have all come down to us from the Greeks of more than two thousand years ago, and had, no doubt, earlier beginnings of which we know little or nothing. The Essay, on the other hand, is a modern form with a modern purpose, and we know not only its date and origin, but the date and origin of its name, with unusual exactness.

It was not long after the death of his father (Pierre Eyquem, who died in 1569) that Michel, Sieur de Montaigne, retired to his Château of Montaigne * with

---

* In Dordogne, some twenty-eight miles from Périgueux.

the intention of writing about himself. The place had drawbacks : the house was too big—it had once taken in the King's Court—the library, though attractive, was small, and the countryside so wild and remote that he had not one neighbour, he says, who could say his *Paternoster* in Latin, or speak any French at all worth the name. But it suited Montaigne's purpose. " I could have written better elsewhere ; but the work would have been less my own : and the principal end and perfection in view is that it should be exactly mine."

The " chapters " of his book are not strictly chapters, but disconnected papers on every kind of subject and of enormously varying length. He eventually gave to the whole collection the title of *Essais :* a word of modesty, meaning that the contents were not serious logically composed discourses or treatises, but merely trial pieces or experiments. It appears that it was he who used the word in its literary sense for the first time ; and we can see him feeling his way towards it in a passage where he is speaking of his friend's book, " Il l'escrivit par manière d'essay, en sa première jeunesse." * This is the earliest example given by Littré of the application of the word to a literary effort ; and when once Montaigne had used it in this way it would be natural enough for him to go further and use it absolutely, as a name for his new form of self-expression. So, when the book appeared, with *Essais* for title, the new form and the new name came into the world together.

This was at Bordeaux in 1580. The edition contained two books, the first of fifty-seven chapters, the second of thirty-seven. To these was added (in the fifth edition, published at Paris in 1588) a third book of thirteen chapters. In the three centuries which followed these hundred odd essays have been so con-

* *Essais*, I., p. 27.

stantly read and so powerful in effect that the type
has become fixed and permanent, in spite of the
changing influences of society, science, and speculation.
Changes have had their effect, but upon the word
" essay " rather than the thing itself. We have for
many years now used the word to include precisely
those longer and more scientific compositions which
Montaigne was careful to disclaim. For such we
might well reserve some other name, better suited to
their more dogmatic nature. We do in fact more often
speak of them as " articles," " papers," " theses,"
" monographs," " studies," " addresses," or even
" lectures " : but when it comes to publishing in
book form, the title of " Essays " is too often usurped
for the sake of its literary prestige.

The essay proper remains, and will always remain,
distinct from all these. Its aim is fundamentally
different. One man may write a series of articles, and
another a series of essays, on subjects nominally the
same : but if the latter are true essays in the Montaigne tradition, the effect of the two books will be
quite unlike—in the one case information, persuasion,
or criticism ; in the other, an autobiography, a confession, or self-portrait. The difference between the
two kinds of writing, the essential quality which places
them on this side or that of the dividing line, is subtly
traced in Conrad's prefatory note to his collection of
Notes on Life and Letters. A good deal of the book
consists of articles or reviews reprinted from period-
icals. But these, in their author's view, are not
simply journalism, or simply criticism—they have for
him a quality which imposes on him the duty of
preserving them. " This, to be frank about it, is a
process of tidying up, which, from the nature of things,
cannot be regarded as premature. The fact is that I
wanted to do it myself, because of a feeling that had
nothing to do with the considerations of worthiness
or unworthiness of the small (but unbroken) pieces

collected within the covers of this volume. Of course it may be said that I might have taken up a broom and used it without saying anything about it. That certainly is one way of tidying up."

The reader will note that this is already a little piece of autobiography, for it was written in 1921, and reveals the author's quiet conviction that his time was short. He sees his work in retrospect, and values it as belonging not to the world's life but to his own. " It would have been too much to have expected me to treat all this matter as removable rubbish. All those things had a place in my life. Whether any of them deserve to have been picked up and ranged on the shelf—this shelf—I cannot say, and frankly, I have not allowed my mind to dwell on the question. I was afraid of thinking myself into a mood that would hurt my feelings : for those pieces of writing, whatever may be the comment on their display, appertain to the character of the man. And so here they are, dusted, which was but a decent thing to do, but in no way polished, extending from the year '98 to the year '20, a thin array (for such a stretch of time) of really innocent attitudes : Conrad literary, Conrad political, Conrad reminiscent, Conrad controversial. Well, yes ! a one-man show—or is it merely the show of one man ?

" The only thing," he goes on, " that will not be found amongst those Figures and Things that have passed away, will be Conrad *en pantoufles*. It is a constitutional inability. *Schlafrock und Pantoffeln !* Not that ! Never ! . . . This volume (including these embarrassed introductory remarks) is as near as I shall ever come to *déshabillé* in public, and perhaps it will do something to help towards a better vision of the man, if it gives no more than a partial view of his back, a little dusty (after the process of tidying up), a little bowed, and receding from the world not because of weariness or misanthropy, but for other reasons that cannot be helped : because the leaves fall, the water flows, the clock ticks with that horrid pitiless solemnity which you must have observed in the ticking of the hall clock at home. For reasons like that. Yes, it recedes. And this was the chance to afford one more view of it,—even to my own eyes . . ."

In another passage he adds some very suggestive reflections which touch on the relation of literature to personal expression. " The part I have ventured, for shortness' sake, to call ' Life,' may perhaps justify itself by the emotional sincerity of the feelings to which the various papers included under that head owe their origin. And as they relate to events of which every one has a date,·they are in the nature of signposts pointing out the direction my thoughts were compelled to take at the various cross-roads. If anybody detects any sort of inconsistency in the choice, this will be only proof positive that wisdom had nothing to do with it. Whether right or wrong. instinct alone is invariable : a fact which only adds a deeper shade to its inherent mystery. The appearance of intellectuality these pieces may present at first sight is merely the result of the arrangement of words. The logic that may be found there is only the logic of the language. But I need not labour the point. There will be plenty of people sagacious enough to perceive the absence of all wisdom from these pages. But I believe sufficiently in human sympathies to imagine that very few will question their sincerity. Whatever delusions I may have suffered from, I have had no delusions as to the nature of the facts commented on here. I may have misjudged their import : but that is the sort of error for which one may expect a certain amount of toleration."

All this, so easily and quickly said, is true, and even profoundly true : it goes to the root, and the longer you look at it the more you see growing out of it.

Where does it all come from ? From Conrad, no doubt : not from the Conrad of the novels, but from a fellow lodger of equal genius, who would scorn to live in a world without significance, and knows that he must look for the source of all values in himself. I cannot say whether he derived directly from the Father of Essays, or only indirectly through the English tradition ; but when I read the passages I have quoted I was impelled to go back to Montaigne's own little Preface.

" Here, Reader, is an honest book. It warns you at the front door that my aim is purely private and domestic. I am not here considering how to serve you or glorify myself ; such a design is beyond my powers. My book is devoted to the particular purposes of my friends and relations : that when they have lost me (which they must do before long) they may find in it some characteristic touches of my temperament and mood, and so keep more complete and more living whatever knowledge they have had of me. If my object had been to seek the world's favour, I should have decked myself with borrowed ornaments. But my wish is to be seen simply in my own fashion, natural and ordinary, unstudied and without artifice : for it is myself that I am painting. Here you will find my faults drawn to the life, my imperfections and my natural form displayed, so far as a regard for public decency permits me. And if I had belonged to one of those Nations who are said to live still under the gentle freedom of the primitive Laws of Nature, I do assure you that I would very willingly have drawn myself entire and naked.

" Thus, Reader, I am myself the subject of my book : but that is no reason why you should spend your leisure on anything so frivolous and worthless. So good-bye."

Consciously or not, the descendant is at one with his ancestor. " Frivolous and worthless : removable rubbish : yet no, all those things had a place in my life, and appertain to the character of the man : they are characteristic touches of my temperament and mood : me literary, me political, me reminiscent, me controversial : and it is myself that I am painting. So far as public decency permits : me in slippers you will never see. But all that will make the portrait lifelike to friends and relations, and even to myself, that shall be put in, faults included, and the domination of instinct rather than wisdom. Unstudied too, and without artifice : any appearance of intellectuality here is only the result of the arrangement of words : the only logic is the logic of the language." It is not easy to distinguish the one voice from the other : they chime together.

For the justification of this egotistic study the two self-painters have slightly different pleas. Montaigne's wish is to be seen as he is, and to be remembered as he was, by those who value him. Conrad asks rather for toleration and a sympathetic recognition of his sincerity. But here, too, they are really at one : both are busy tidying up for those who come after—a process which is not premature, for both know that they must go before long. And neither of them cares to give the real reason—that he writes to realize himself, and knows the pleasure which he will give to the rest of mankind, who like himself love the colour of personality even more than the marble contours of art. I do not forget that " the rest of mankind" included some stern exceptions. Dr. Johnson, for example, says of Sir Thomas Browne and his *Religio Medici*, " It indeed contains many passages, which, relating merely to his own person, can be of no great importance to the publick : but when it was written it happened to him as to others—he was too much pleased with his performance, not to think it might please others as much." But here King Critic has not carried conviction : it is just because the book was in all its passages an account of the physician's own religion, a personal view, that it has appeared of so great importance to the public through two and a half centuries.

Not only to the public, but to a long line of writers, a company which continues to increase. Even in a small collection like ours this comes out clearly. Bacon, Cowley, and Leigh Hunt confess their descent by the incidental mention of Montaigne's name. Addison and Hewlett go farther, and write whole essays on Montaigne and on others of his following. Equally significant is the recognition by many of the rest that they are mainly concerned with themselves, that they are their own subject. Cowley writes boldly, " On Myself " : Hewlett confessedly on his own misgivings between journalism and literature. Others are equally conscious of their " noble egotism," but are forced by a feeling of delicacy to throw a slight veil over it. Their forms of camouflage are amusingly varied. Lamb at his most autobiographical pretends to be a schoolfellow of " Mr. Lamb," or " a friend of the late Elia." Others, may we say, like ostriches, seek to hide their presence by burying their " I." Mr. Belloc covers his own head with " a man " or " one " : Mr. Edward Thomas uses " we " in personal remininiscences : Arthur Clutton-Brock also attributes his own taste to a plural critic : Mr. Gilbert Chesterton describes himself as " every one of us in childhood " : and Mrs. Meynell, speaking all the time in her own unmistakable voice, wears the costume of " He who " or " The man." All these are easy and effective ways of averting, not recognition or criticism, but the pain of self-assertion. In this matter Stevenson goes to the other extreme, and there can be no doubt that his generation liked him for it : the more he asserted himself the more pleasure he gave. Bacon and Cowley perhaps hit the happy mean : they use the " I " with as much naturalness as if they were writing a private letter.

Maurice Hewlett has an interesting passage in which he defines the Essay, and points out some of its demands and limitations. " If one had to define an Essay it would be as the written, after-dinner monologue of a well-read, well-satisfied man of, at least, five and forty. Years don't matter : the spirit of years matters very much. You must be mature enough to pontificate, and wise enough to do it tact-fully . . ." Then come the limitations. " You must not be long, you should not be difficult ; you may be discursive but not abrupt . . . you may not take sides, nor improve the occasion. Your teaching must be by the way. ' Je n'enseigne point," Montaigne says, ' je raconte.' You will be allusive, of course : all full men are so ; and you will quote freely, often inaccurately. Anecdote should be your salt, but I don't think quotation should be your pepper."

A glance through our collection will confirm this and illustrate it. It will show that there are certain lines—not very many—on which the object of self-revelation may be pursued with success. There must be nothing like systematic biography : but personal experiences, reminiscences, and anecdotes will be found in almost every essay. Lamb used reminis-cence very often as the professed form of his essay : Cowley and Steele more incidentally. Edward Thomas's essay here given is pure reminiscence. Bacon's on *Masques and Triumphs* reads to me as reminiscent throughout : he must have seen and even directed many such " toys." Personal tastes give the essayist another chance : gardens for Bacon and Goldsmith ; "littleness" for Cowley ; old china for Lamb ; style for John Addington Symonds and Arthur Clutton-Brock ; books for Leigh Hunt, Hazlitt, and others ; journeys and houses for Stevenson and Mary

Coleridge : and the two last have both written also on books, and spun fine patterns out of memory. These are the chief threads which lie ready for the essayist's loom : stouter ones he must in general avoid. But Mr. Lynd has, like Goldsmith, the art of writing reminiscences which are also fragments of history, as may be seen in his *Darkness* and others of the volume from which it comes.

PUBLISHERS' NOTE

Acknowledgments for the use of copyright material are due and are hereby tendered to : Mr. G. K. Chesterton and Messrs. J. M. Dent & Sons, Ltd., for *A Defence of Penny Dreadfuls* ; Mr. John Murray for *Personal Style*, by John Addington Symonds ; Messrs. Duckworth & Co. for *Broken Memories*, by Edward Thomas ; Messrs. Chatto and Windus for *Random Memories* and *The Ideal House*, by R. L. Stevenson ; Mr. Hilaire Belloc and Messrs. Methuen & Co., Ltd., for *Our Inheritance* ; Mrs. Clutton - Brock and Messrs. Methuen & Co., Ltd., for *The Defects of English Prose* ; Mr. Robert Lynd for *The Darkness* ; the executors of the late Maurice Hewlett and the Oxford University Press for *The Maypole and the Column* and *Montaigne* ; and the executors of Mary E. Coleridge for *Gifts, On Paper Matches*, and *The Drawing-Room*.

ESSAYS AND ESSAYISTS

MONTAIGNE (Florio's Translation)

Of Idlenesse

As we see some idle-fallow grounds, if they be fat and
fertile, to bring foorth store and sundry roots of wilde
and unprofitable weeds, and that to keep them in ure
we must subject and imploy them with certain seeds
for our use and service; so is it of mindes, which except
they be busied about some subject, that may bridle
and keepe them under, they will here and there
wildely scatter themselves through the vast field of
imaginations.

> *Sicut aquæ tremulum labris ubi lumen ahenis*
> *Sole repercussum, aut radiantis imagine Lunæ,*
> *Omnia pervolitat latè loca, jamque sub auras*
> *Erigitur, summique ferit laquearia tecti.*

> As trembling light reflected from the Sunne,
> Or radiant Moone on water-fild brasse lavers,
> Flies over all, in aire upraisèd soone,
> Strikes house-top beames, betwixt both strangely
>   wavers.

And there is no folly, or extravagant raving, they
produce not in that agitation.

In ure, At work.

——— *velut ægri somnia, vanæ*
Finguntur species.

Like sicke mens dreames, that feigne
Imaginations vaine.

The minde that hath no fixed bound, will easily
loose itselfe : For, as we say, " To be everiewhere, is
to be nowhere."

Quisquis ubique habitat, Maxime, nusquam habitat.

Good sir, he that dwels everywhere,
No where can say, that he dwels there.

It is not long since I retired myselfe unto mine
owne house, with full purpose, as much as lay in me,
not to trouble myselfe with any businesse, but soli-
tarily and quietly to weare out the remainder of my
well-nigh-spent life ; where me thought I could doe
my spirit no greater favour, than to give him the full
scope of idlenesse, and entertaine him as he best
pleased, and withall, to settle himselfe as he best
liked : which I hoped he might now, being by time
become more setled and ripe, accomplish very easily :
but I finde,

Variam semper dant otia mentem.

Evermore idlenesse,
Doth wavering mindes addresse.

That contrariwise playing the skittish and loose-
broken jade, he takes a hundred times more cariere
and libertie unto himselfe, than hee did for others,
and begets in me so many extravagant Chimeraes, and

Evermore idlenesse, etc., or more accurately,—
Idlenesse every way
Maketh the mind to stray.
Cariere, Full gallop.

fantasticall monsters, so orderlesse, and without any
reason, one hudling upon another, that at leasure to
view the foolishnesse and monstrous strangenesse of
them, I have begun to keepe a register of them, hoping, if I live, one day to make him ashamed, and
blush at himselfe.

Of Readie or Slow Speech

Onc ne furent à tous toutes graces données.

All God's good graces are not gone
To all, or of all any one.

So doe we see that in the gift of eloquence, some have
such a facility and promptitude, and that which we
call utterance, so easie and at command, that at all
assaies, and upon everie occasion, they are ready and
provided ; and others more slow, never speake anything except much laboured and premeditated, as
Ladies and daintie Dames are taught rules to take
recreations and bodily exercises, according to the
advantage of what they have fairest about them.   If
I were to give the like counsel, in those two different
advantages of eloquence whereof Preachers and plead-
ing-lawiers of our age seeme to make profession ; the
slow speaker in mine opinion should be the better
preacher, and the other the better lawier.   Forsomuch as charge of the first allowes him as much leisure
as he pleaseth to prepare himselfe ; moreover his
cariere continueth still in one kinde without inter-
ruption : whereas the Lawyers occasions urging him
still upon any accident to be ready to enter the lists :
and the unexpected replies and answers of his adverse
partie, do often divert him from his purpose, wher he
is enforced to take a new course.   Yet is it, that at

Assaies, Trials.   *Charge*, The business.

the last enterview which was at Marseilles betweene
Pope Clement the seventh, and Francis the first, our
King, it hapned cleane contrarie, where Monsieur
Poyet, a man of chiefe reputation, and all dayes of
his life brought up to plead at the bar, whose charge
being to make an Oration before the Pope, and having
long time before premeditated and con'd the same by
roat, yea, and as some report, brought it with him
ready penned from Paris; the very same day it should
have beene pronounced; the Pope suspecting he
might haply speak something, might offend the other
Princes Ambassadors, that were about him, sent the
argument, which he at that time and place thought
fittest to be treated of, to the King, but by fortune
cleane contrarie to that which Poyet had so much
studied for: So that his Oration was altogether frus-
trate, and he must presently frame another. But he
perceiving himselfe unable for it, the Cardinall Bellay
was faine to supply his place and take that charge upon
him. The Lawyers charge is much harder than the
Preachers: yet in mine opinion shall we find more
passable Lawyers than commendable Preachers, at
least in France. It seemeth to be more proper to the
mind to have her operation ready and sudden, and
more incident to the judgement to have it slow and
considerate. But who remaineth mute, if he have
no leisure to prepare himselfe, and he likewise to
whom leisure giveth no advantage to say better, are
both in one selfe degree of strangenesse. It is reported that Severus Cassius spake better extempore,
and without premeditation. That he was more beholding to fortune, than to his diligence; that to be
interrupted in his speech redounded to his profit:
and that his adversaries feared to urge him, lest his
sudden anger should redouble his eloquence. I know
this condition of nature by experience, which cannot

In one selfe, In the self same.

abide a vehement and laborious premeditation : except it hold a free, a voluntarie, and selfe pleasing course, it can never come to a good end. We commonly say of some compositions, that they smell of the oile, and of the lampe, by reason of a certaine harshnesse, and rudenesse, which long plodding labour imprints in them that be much elaborated. But besides, the care of well-doing, and the contention of the minde, overstretched to her enterprise, doth breake and impeach the same ; even as it hapneth unto water, which being closely pent in, through its owne violence and abundance, cannot finde issue at an open gullet. In this condition of nature, whereof I now speake, this also is joyned unto it, that it desireth not to be pricked forward by these strong passions, as the anger of Cassius (for that motion would be overrude) it ought not to be violently shaken, but yeeldingly solicited : it desireth to be rouzed and prickt forward by strange occasions, both present and casuall. If it goe all alone, it doth but languish and loyter behinde : agitation is her life and grace. I cannot well containe myselfe in mine owne possession and disposition, chance hath more interest in it than myselfe ; occasion, company, yea the change of my voice, drawes more from my minde than I can finde therein, when by myselfe I second and endevor to employ the same. My words likewise are better than my writings, if choice may be had in so worthlesse things. This also hapneth unto me, that where I seeke myselfe, I finde not myselfe : and I finde myselfe more by chance, than by the search of mine owne judgement. I shall perhaps have cast foorth some suttletie in writing, haply dull and harsh for another, but smooth and curious for myselfe. Let us leave all these complements and quaintnesse. That is spoken by everie man, according to his owne strength. I have so lost it, that I wot not what I would have said, and strangers have sometimes found it before me. Had I alwayes a razor about me, where that hapneth, I should cleane raze myselfe out. Fortune may at some other time make the light thereof appeare brighter unto me than that of mid-day, and will make mee wonder at mine owne faltring or sticking in the myre.

Of Constancie

THE law of resolution and constancie implieth not, we should not, as much as lieth in our power, shelter our selves from the mischiefes and inconveniences that threaten us, nor by consequence feare they should surprise us. Contrariwise, all honest meanes for a man to warrant himselfe from evils are not onely tolerable, but commendable. And the part of constancie is chiefly acted, in firmely bearing the inconveniences, against which no remedie is to be found. So that there is no nimblenesse of bodie, nor wealding of hand-weapons, that we will reject, if it may in any sort defend us from the blow, meant at us. Many most warlike nations in their conflicts and fights, used retreating and flight as a principall advantage, and shewed their backs to their enemie much more dangerously than their faces. The Turkes at this day retaine something of that humour. And Socrates in Plato doth mocke at Laches, because he had defined fortitude, to keepe herselfe steadie in her rancke against her enemies ; " What," saith hee, " were it then cowardise to beat them in giving them place ? " And alleageth Homer against him, who commendeth in Æneas his skill in flying and giving ground. And because Laches being better advised, avoweth that custome to be amongst the Scithians, and generally amongst all horsemen, he alleageth further unto him the example of the Lacedemonian footmen (a nation above all other used to fight on foot) who in the battell of

Plateæ, unable to open and to put to rowt the Persian
Phalanx, advised themselves to scatter and put themselves backe, that so by the opinion of their flight,
they might if they should pursue them, rush in upon
them, and put that so combined-masse to rout. By
which meanes they gained the victorie. Touching the
Scithians, it is reported, that when Darius went to
subdue them, he sent their King many reprochfull
speeches, for so much as hee ever saw him retire and
give ground before him, and to avoid the maine battell. To whom Indathirsez (for so was his name)
answered, that " They did it not for feare of him, nor
any other man living, but that it was the fashion of
his nation to march thus : as having neither cities,
nor houses, nor manured land to defend, or to feare
their enemies should reape any commoditie by them."
But if hee had so great a desire to feed on them, he
might draw neerer to view the place of their ancient
Sepulchers, and there hee should meet with whom to
speake his belly-full. Notwithstanding when a man
is once within reach of cannon-shot, and as it were
point-blancke before them, as the fortune of warre
doth diverse times bring men unto, it ill beseemeth a
resolute minde to start-aside, or be daunted at the
threat of a shot, because by the violence and sudden-
nesse thereof wee deeme it inevitable : and there are
some, who by lifting up of a hand, or stooping their
head, have sometimes given their fellowes cause of
laughter : yet have we seene, that in the voyage the
Emperour Charles the fifth made against us in Provence, the Marquis of Guasto, being gone out to survey
the citie of Arles, and shewne himselfe out of a winde-
mill, under colour of which he was come somewhat
neere the Towne, he was discovered by the Lord of
Bonevall, and the Seneshall of Agenois, who were
walking upon the Theatre Aux arenes (so called in
French because it is full of sand) who shewing him to
the Lord of Villiers, Commissarie of the Artillerie, hee

mounted a culverin so levell, that had not the Marquis
perceived the fire, and so started aside, it was constantly affirmed, hee had beene shot through the body.
Likewise not many yeeres before, Lorence of Medicis,
Duke of Vrbin, and father to the Queene-mother of
France, besieging Mondolphe, a place in Italie, in the
province name Vicariate, seeing fire given to a piece
that stood upright upon him, stooped his head, and
well befell him that he plaide the ducke, for otherwise
the bullet, which went right over, and within a little
of his head, had doubtlesse shot him through the
paunch.   But to say truth, I will never thinke these
motions were made with discourse, for what judgement can you give of an aime, either high or low, in
a matter so sudden ?   It may rather be thought that
fortune favoured their feare : and which an other
time might as well bee a meane to make them fall
into the cannons-mouth, as to avoid the same.   I cannot chuse, if the cracke of a musket doe suddenly
streeke mine eares, in a place where I least looke for
it, but I must needs start at it : which I have seene
happen to men of better sort than my selfe.   Nor doe
the Stoickes meane, that the Soule of their wisest man
in any sort resist the first visions and sudden fantasies,
that surprise the same : but rather consent that, as it
were unto a naturall subjection, he yeelds and shrinks
unto the loud clattering and roare of heaven, or of
some violent downefall ; for example-sake, unto pale-
nesse, and contraction.   So likewise in other passions,
alwayes provided his opinion remaines safe and whole,
and the situation of his reason admit no tainting or
alteration whatsoever : and hee no whit consent to
his fright and sufferance.   Touching the first part ;
the same hapneth to him, that is not wise, but farre
otherwise concerning the second.   For the impression
of passions doth not remaine superficiall in him : but

Name, Named.   *With discourse*, Deliberately.

rather penetrates even into the secret of reason, infecting and corrupting the same. He judgeth according to them, and conformeth himselfe to them. Consider precisely the state of the wise Stoicke :

Mens immota manet, lachrymæ volvuntur inanes.

> His minde doth firme remaine,
> Teares are distill'd in vaine.

The wise Peripatetike doth not exempt himselfe from perturbations of the mind, but doth moderate them.

That We should not Judge of Our Happinesse untill after Our Death

> ———— *scilicet ultima semper*
> *Expectanda dies homini est, dicique beatus*
> *Ante obitum nemo, supremaque funera debet.*

> We must expect of man the latest day,
> Nor ere he die, he's happie, can we say.

THE very children are acquainted with the storie of Crœsus to this purpose : who being taken by Cyrus, and by him condemned to die, upon the point of his execution, cried out aloud : "Oh Solon, Solon!" which words of his, being reported to Cyrus, who inquiring what he meant by them, told him, hee now at his owne cost verified the advertisement Solon had before times given him ; which was, that no man, what cheerefull and blandishing countenance soever fortune shewed them, may rightly deeme himselfe happie, till such time as he have passed the last day of his life, by reason of the uncertaintie and vicissitude of humane things, which by a very light motive, and slight occasion, are often changed from one to another

Secret, Secret chamber.　　　*Advertisement*, Instruction.

cleane contrary state and degree. And therefore Agesilaus answered one that counted the King of Persia happy, because being very young, he had gotten the garland of so mightie and great a dominion : " yea but said he, Priam at the same age was not unhappy." Of the Kings of Macedon that succeeded Alexander the Great, some were afterward seene to become Joyners and Scriveners at Rome : and of Tyrants of Sicilie, Schoolemasters at Corinth. One that had conquered halfe the world, and been Emperour over so many Armies, became an humble and miserable suter to the raskally officers of a king of Ægypte : At so high a rate did that great Pompey purchase the irkesome prolonging of his life but for five or six moneths. And in our fathers daies, Lodowicke Sforze, tenth Duke of Millane, under whom the State of Italie had so long beene turmoiled and shaken, was seene to die a wretched prisoner at Loches in France, but not till he had lived and lingered ten yeares in thraldom, which was the worst of his bargaine. The fairest Queene, wife to the greatest King of Christendome, was she not lately seene to die by the hands of an executioner ? Oh unworthie and barbarous crueltie ! And a thousand such examples. For, it seemeth that as the sea-billowes and surging waves, rage and storme against the surly pride and stubborne height of our buildings, so are there above, certaine spirits that envie the rising prosperities and greatnesse heere below.

> *Vsque adeò res humanas vis abdita quædam*
> *Obierit, et pulchros fasces sævásque secures*
> *Proculcare, ac ludibrio sibi habere videtur.*

A hidden power so mens states hath out-worne
Faire swords, fierce scepters, signes of honours borne,
It seemes to trample and deride in scorne.

And it seemeth Fortune doth sometimes narrowly watch the last day of our life, thereby to shew her power, and in one moment to overthrow what for many yeares together she had been erecting, and makes us cry after Laberius, *Nimirum hac die unâ plus vixi, mihi quam vivendum fuit.* Thus it is, " I have lived longer by this one day than I should." So may that good advice of Solon be taken with reason. But forsomuch as he is a Philosopher, with whom the favours or disfavours of fortune, and good or ill lucke have no place, and are not regarded by him ; and puissances and greatnesses, and accidents of qualitie, are wellnigh indifferent : I deeme it very likely he had a further reach, and meant that the same good fortune of our life, which dependeth of the tranquillitie and contentment of a welborne minde, and of the resolution and assurance of a well ordered soule, should never be ascribed unto man, untill he have beene seene play the last act of his comedie, and without doubt the hardest. In all the rest there may be some maske : either these sophisticall discourses of Philosophie are not in us but by countenance, or accidents that never touch us to the quick give us alwaies leasure to keep our countenance setled. But when that last part of death, and of our selves comes to be acted, then no dissembling will availe, then is it high time to speake plaine English, and put off all vizards : then whatsoever the pot containeth must be shewne, be it good or bad, foule or cleane, wine or water.

Nam veræ voces tum demum pectore ab imo
Ejiciuntur, et eripitur persona, manet res.

For then are sent true speeches from the heart,
We are ourselves, we leave to play a part.

Loe heere, why at this last cast, all our lives other actions must be tride and touched. It is the masterday, the day that judgeth all others : it is the day, saith an aunciet Writer, that must judge of all my

Countenance, The looks we put on.   *Vizards*, masks.

forepassed yeares. To death doe I referre the essay
of my studies fruit. There shall wee see whether my
discourse proceed from my heart, or from my mouth.
I have seene divers, by their death, either in good or
evill, give reputation to all their forepassed life. Scipio,
father-in-law to Pompey, in well dying, repaired the ill
opinion which untill that houre men had ever held of
him. Epaminondas being demanded which of the
three he esteemed most, either Chabrias, or Iphicrates,
or himselfe: "It is necessary," said he, "that we be
seene to die, before your question may well be resolved." Verily, we should steale much from him,
if he should be weighed without the honour and greatnesse of his end. God hath willed it, as he pleased:
but in my time three of the most execrable persons
that ever I knew in all abomination of life, and the
most infamous, have beene seene to die very orderly
and quietly, and in every circumstance composed
even unto perfection. There are some brave and
fortunate deaths. I have seene her cut the twine of
some man's life, with a progresse of wonderful ad-
vancement, and with so worthie an end, even in the
flowre of his growth and spring of his youth, that in
mine opinion, his ambitious and haughtie couragious
designes, thought nothing so high as might interrupt
them: who without going to the place where he
pretended, arived there more gloriously and worthily
than either his desire or hope aimed at, and by his
fall fore-went the power and name, whither by his
course he aspired. When I judge of other men's lives,
I ever respect how they have behaved themselves in
their end; and my chiefest study is, I may well de-
meane my selfe at my last gaspe, that is to say, quietly
and constantly.

Essay, Trial (assay). *Her*, Death (La Mort).
Fore-went, Went beyond. *Respect*, Observe.

FRANCIS BACON

Of Truth

What is truth? said jesting Pilate, and would not stay
for an answer. Certainly there be that delight in
giddiness, and count it a bondage to fix a belief ;
affecting free-will in thinking, as well as in acting.
And though the sects of philosophers of that kind be
gone, yet there remain certain discoursing wits which
are of the same veins, though there be not so much
blood in them as was in those of the ancients. But
it is not only the difficulty and labour which men
take in finding out of truth, nor again that when it is
found it imposeth upon men's thoughts, that doth
bring lies in favour ; but a natural though corrupt
love of the lie itself. One of the later school of the
Grecians examineth the matter, and is at a stand to
think what should be in it, that men should love lies ;
where neither they make for pleasure, as with poets ;
nor for advantage, as with the merchant ; but for
the lie's sake. But I cannot tell : this same truth
is a naked and open day-light, that doth not shew
the masques and mummeries and triumphs of the
world, half so stately and daintily as candle-lights.
Truth may perhaps come to the price of a pearl, that
sheweth best by day ; but it will not rise to the price
of a diamond or carbuncle, that sheweth best in
varied lights. A mixture of a lie doth ever add
pleasure. Doth any man doubt, that if there were
taken out of men's minds vain opinions, flattering
hopes, false valuations, imaginations as one would,

and the like, but it would leave the minds of a number of men poor shrunken things, full of melancholy and indisposition, and unpleasing to themselves? One of the fathers, in great severity, called poesy *vinum dæmonum*, because it filleth the imagination, and yet it is but with the shadow of a lie. But it is not the lie that passeth through the mind, but the lie that sinketh in and settleth in it, that doth the hurt, such as we spake of before. But howsoever these things are thus in men's depraved judgments and affections, yet truth, which only doth judge itself, teacheth that the inquiry of truth, which is the love-making or wooing of it, the knowledge of truth, which is the presence of it, and the belief of truth, which is the enjoying of it, is the sovereign good of human nature. The first creature of God, in the works of the days, was the light of the sense; the last was the light of reason; and his sabbath work, ever since, is the illumination of his Spirit. First he breathed light upon the face of the matter or chaos; then he breathed light into the face of man; and still he breatheth and inspireth light into the face of his chosen. The poet that beautified the sect that was otherwise inferior to the rest, saith yet excellently well: *It is a pleasure to stand upon the shore, and to see ships tost upon the sea: a pleasure to stand in the window of a castle, and to see a battle and the adventures thereof below: but no pleasure is comparable to the standing upon the vantage ground of truth* (a hill not to be commanded, and where the air is always clear and serene), *and to see the errors, and wanderings, and mists, and tempests, in the vale below:* so always that this prospect be with pity, and not with swelling or pride. Certainly, it is heaven upon earth, to have a man's mind move in charity, rest in providence, and turn upon the poles of truth.

Vinum dæmonum, The wine of devils.

To pass from theological and philosophical truth, to the truth of civil business : it will be acknowledged, even by those that practise it not, that clear and round dealing is the honour of man's nature ; and that mixture of falsehood is like allay in coin of gold and silver ; which may make the metal work the better, but it embaseth it. For these winding and crooked courses are the goings of the serpent ; which goeth basely upon the belly, and not upon the feet. There is no vice that doth so cover a man with shame as to be found false and perfidious. And therefore Mountaigny saith prettily, when he inquired the reason, why the word of the lie should be such a disgrace and such an odious charge ? saith he, *If it be well weighed, to say that a man lieth, is as much to say as that he is brave towards God and a coward towards men.* For a lie faces God, and shrinks from man. Surely the wickedness of falsehood and breach of faith cannot possibly be so highly expressed, as in that it shall be the last peal to call the judgments of God upon the generations of men ; it being foretold, that when Christ cometh, *he shall not find faith upon the earth.*

Of Wisdom for a Man's Self

AN ant is a wise creature for itself, but it is a shrewd thing in an orchard or garden. And certainly men that are great lovers of themselves waste the public. Divide with reason between self-love and society ; and be so true to thyself, as thou be not false to others, specially to thy king and country. It is a poor centre of a man's actions, himself. It is right earth. For that only stands fast upon his own centre ; whereas all things that have affinity with the heavens move upon the centre of another, which they benefit. The

Shrewd, Cursed.

referring of all to a man's self is more tolerable in a
sovereign prince ; because themselves are not only
themselves, but their good and evil is at the peril of
the public fortune. But it is a desperate evil in a
servant to a prince, or a citizen in a republic. For
whatsoever affairs pass such a man's hands, he
crooketh them to his own ends ; which must needs
be often eccentric to the ends of his master or state.
Therefore let princes, or states, choose such servants
as have not this mark ; except they mean their
service should be made but the accessary. That
which maketh the effect more pernicious is that all
proportion is lost. It were disproportion enough for
the servant's good to be preferred before the master's ;
but yet it is a greater extreme, when a little good of
the servant shall carry things against a great good
of the master's. And yet that is the case of bad
officers, treasurers, ambassadors, generals, and other
false and corrupt servants ; which set a bias upon
their bowl, of their own petty ends and envies, to
the overthrow of their master's great and important
affairs. And for the most part, the good such servants receive is after the model of their own fortune ;
but the hurt they sell for that good is after the model
of their master's fortune. And certainly it is the
nature of extreme self-lovers, as they will set an house
on fire, and it were but to roast their eggs ; and yet
these men many times hold credit with their masters,
because their study is but to please them and profit
themselves ; and for either respect they will abandon
the good of their affairs.

Wisdom for a man's self is, in many branches thereof, a depraved thing. It is the wisdom of rats, that
will be sure to leave a house somewhat before it fall.
It is the wisdom of the fox, that thrusts out the badger,
who digged and made room for him. It is the wis-

Eccentric to, Inconsistent with.
After the model, In proportion to.

dom of crocodiles, that shed tears when they would devour. But that which is specially to be noted is, that those which (as Cicero says of Pompey) are *sui amantes sine rivali*, are many times unfortunate. And whereas they have all their time sacrificed to themselves, they become in the end themselves sacrifices to the inconstancy of fortune, whose wings they thought by their self-wisdom to have pinioned.

Of Masques and Triumphs

THESE things are but toys, to come amongst such serious observations. But yet, since princes will have such things, it is better they should be graced with elegancy, than daubed with cost. Dancing to song is a thing of great state and pleasure. I understand it, that the song be in quire, placed aloft, and accompanied with some broken music; and the ditty fitted to the device. Acting in song, especially in dialogues, hath an extreme good grace: I say acting, not dancing (for that is a mean and vulgar thing); and the voices of the dialogue would be strong and manly (a bass and a tenor, no treble); and the ditty high and tragical, not nice or dainty. Several quires, placed one over against another, and taking the voice by catches, anthem-wise, give great pleasure. Turning dances into figure is a childish curiosity. And generally, let it be noted, that those things which I here set down are such as do naturally take the sense, and not respect petty wonderments. It is true, the alterations of scenes, so it be quietly and without noise, are things of great beauty and pleasure; for they feed and relieve the eye, before it be full of the same object. Let the scenes abound with light, specially coloured and varied; and let the masquers, or any

Sui amantes sine rivali, Men who love themselves without a rival.
Take, Captivate.   *Respect*, aim at.

other, that are to come down from the scene, have some motions upon the scene itself before their coming down ; for it draws the eye strangely, and makes it with great pleasure to desire to see that it cannot perfectly discern. Let the songs be loud and cheerful, and not chirpings or pulings. Let the music likewise be sharp and loud and well placed. The colours that shew best by candle-light are white, carnation, and a kind of sea-water-green ; and oes, or spangs, as they are of no great cost, so they are of most glory. As for rich embroidery, it is lost and not discerned. Let the suits of the masquers be graceful, and such as become the person when the vizars are off : not after examples of known attires ; Turks, soldiers, mariners, and the like. Let antimasques not be long ; they have been commonly of fools, satyrs, baboons, wild-men, antics, beasts, sprites, witches, Ethiopes, pigmies, turquets, nymphs, rustics, Cupids, statuas moving, and the like. As for angels, it is not comical enough to put them in antimasques ; and any thing that is hideous, as devils, giants, is on the other side as unfit. But chiefly, let the music of them be recreative, and with some strange changes. Some sweet odours, suddenly coming forth, without any drops falling, are, in such a company as there is steam and heat, things of great pleasure and refreshment. Double masques, one of men, another of ladies, addeth state and variety. But all is nothing, except the room be kept clear and neat.

For justs, and tourneys, and barriers ; the glories of them are chiefly in the chariots, wherein the challengers make their entry ; especially if they be drawn with strange beasts, as lions, bears, camels, and the like ; or in the devices of their entrance ; or in the bravery of their liveries ; or in the goodly

Oes, Round spangles.　　*Antimasques*, Grotesque interludes.
Turquets, Turkish puppets.

furniture of their horses and armour.   But enough of
these toys.

Of Gardens

GOD ALMIGHTY first planted a garden.   And indeed
it is the purest of human pleasures.   It is the greatest
refreshment to the spirits of man ; without which,
buildings and palaces are but gross handyworks :
and a man shall ever see that when ages grow to
civility and elegancy, men come to build stately
sooner than to garden finely ; as if gardening were
the greater perfection.   I do hold it, in the royal
ordering of gardens, there ought to be gardens for
all the months in the year ; in which, severally,
things of beauty may be then in season.   For December and January and the latter part of November,
you must take such things as are green all winter :
holly ; ivy ; bays ; junipers ; cypress-trees ; yew ;
pine-apple-trees ; fir-trees ; rosemary ; lavender ;
periwinkle, the white, the purple, and the blue ;
germander ; flags ; orange-trees, lemon-trees, and
myrtles, if they be stoved ; and sweet marjoram,
warm set.   There followeth, for the latter part of
January and February, the mezereon-tree, which
then blossoms ; crocus vernus, both the yellow and
the grey ; primroses ; anemones ; the early tulippa ;
hyacinthus orientalis ; chamaïris ; fritillaria.   For
March, there come violets, specially the single blue,
which are the earliest ; the yellow daffadil ; the
daisy ; the almond-tree in blossom ; the peach-tree
in blossom ; the cornelian-tree in blossom ; sweet-
briar.   In April follow, the double white violet ; the
wall-flower ; the stock-gillyflower ; the cowslip ;
flower-delices, and lilies of all natures ; rosemary

Stoved, hot-housed.   *Mezereon*, Olive spurge.
        Chamaïris, Dwarf iris.

flowers; the tulippa; the double piony; the pale
daffadil; the French honeysuckle; the cherry-tree
in blossom; the dammasin and plum-trees in blossom; the white-thorn in leaf; the lilac-tree. In
May and June come pinks of all sorts, specially the
blush pink; roses of all kinds, except the musk,
which comes later; honeysuckles; strawberries;
bugloss; columbine; the French marygold; flos
Africanus; cherry-tree in fruit; ribes; figs in fruit;
rasps; vine flowers; lavender in flowers; the sweet
satyrian, with the white flower; herba muscaria;
lilium convallium; the apple-tree in blossom. In
July come gillyflowers of all varieties; musk-roses;
the lime-tree in blossom; early pears and plums in
fruit; ginnitings; quadlins. In August come plums
of all sorts in fruit; pears; apricocks; berberries;
filberds; musk-melons; monks-hoods, of all colours.
In September come grapes; apples; poppies of all
colours; peaches; melocotones; nectarines; cor-
nelians; wardens; quinces. In October and the
beginning of November come services; medlars;
bullises; roses cut or removed to come late; holly-
okes; and such like. These particulars are for the
climate of London; but my meaning is perceived,
that you may have *ver perpetuum*, as the place
affords.

And because the breath of flowers is far sweeter in
the air (where it comes and goes, like the warbling of
music) than in the hand, therefore nothing is more fit
for that delight, than to know what be the flowers and
plants that do best perfume the air. Roses, damask
and red, are fast flowers of their smells; so that you
may walk by a whole row of them, and find nothing of
their sweetness; yea, though it be in a morning's dew.

Satyrian, Orchis.
Quadlins, Codlings.
Cornelian, A kind of cherry.
Ginnitings, Early apples.
Melocotone, A kind of peach.
Ver perpetuum, perpetual Spring.
Fast, Close.

Bays likewise yield no smell as they grow. Rosemary little ; nor sweet marjoram. That which above all others yields the sweetest smell in the air, is the violet ; specially the white double violet, which comes twice a year ; about the middle of April, and about Bartholomewtide. Next to that is the musk-rose. Then the strawberry-leaves dying, which [yield] a most excellent cordial smell. Then the flower of the vines ; it is a little dust, like the dust of a bent, which grows upon the cluster in the first coming forth. Then sweet-briar. Then wall-flowers, which are very delightful to be set under a parlour or lower chamber window. Then pinks and gillyflowers, specially the matted pink and clove gillyflower. Then the flowers of the lime-tree. Then the honey-suckles, so they be somewhat afar off. Of bean flowers I speak not, because they are field flowers. But those which perfume the air most delightfully, not passed by as the rest, but being trodden upon and crushed, are three : that is, burnet, wild thyme, and water-mints. Therefore you are to set whole alleys of them, to have the pleasure when you walk or tread.

For gardens (speaking of those which are indeed prince-like, as we have done of buildings), the contents ought not well to be under thirty acres of ground, and to be divided into three parts : a green in the entrance ; a heath or desert in the going forth ; and the main garden in the midst ; besides alleys on both sides. And I like well that four acres of ground be assigned to the green ; six to the heath ; four and four to either side ; and twelve to the main garden. The green hath two pleasures : the one, because nothing is more pleasant to the eye than green grass kept finely shorn ; the other, because it will give you a fair alley in the midst, by which you may go in front upon a stately hedge, which is to enclose the garden. But because the alley will be long, and, in great heat of the year or day, you ought not to buy the shade in the garden by going in the sun thorough the green, therefore you are, of either side the green, to plant a covert alley, upon carpenter's work, about twelve foot in height, by which you may go in shade into the garden. As for the making of knots or figures with divers-coloured earths, that they may lie under the windows of the house on that side which the garden stands, they be but toys : you may see as good sights many times in tarts. The garden is best to be square ; encompassed, on all the four sides, with a stately arched hedge. The arches to be upon pillars of carpenter's work, of some ten foot high and six foot broad ; and the spaces between of the same dimension with the breadth of the arch. Over the arches let there be an entire hedge, of some four foot high, framed also upon carpenter's work ; and upon the upper hedge, over every arch, a little turret, with a belly, enough to receive a cage of birds ; and over every space between the arches some other little figure, with broad plates of round coloured glass, gilt, for the sun to play upon. But this hedge I intend to be raised upon a bank, not steep, but gently slope, of some six foot, set all with flowers. Also I understand that this square of the garden should not be the whole breadth of the ground, but to leave, on either side, ground enough for diversity of side alleys ; unto which the two covert alleys of the green may deliver you. But there must be no alleys with hedges at either end of this great enclosure : not at the hither end, for letting your prospect upon this fair hedge from the green ; nor at the further end, for letting your prospect from the hedge, through the arches, upon the heath.

For the ordering of the ground within the great hedge, I leave it to variety of device ; advising, never-

Deliver you, Bring you out.   *Letting*, Hindering.

theless, that whatsoever form you cast it into, first, it
be not too busy or full of work. Wherein I, for my
part, do not like images cut out in juniper or other
garden stuff ; they be for children. Little low hedges,
round, like welts, with some pretty pyramides, I like
well ; and in some places, fair columns upon frames
of carpenter's work. I would also have the alleys
spacious and fair. You may have closer alleys upon
the side grounds, but none in the main garden. I
wish also, in the very middle, a fair mount, with three
ascents, and alleys, enough for four to walk abreast ;
which I would have to be perfect circles, without any
bulwarks or embossments ; and the whole mount to
be thirty foot high ; and some fine banqueting-house,
with some chimneys neatly cast, and without too
much glass.

For fountains, they are a great beauty and refreshment ; but pools mar all, and make the garden un-
wholesome and full of flies and frogs. Fountains I
intend to be of two natures : the one, that sprinkleth
or spouteth water ; the other, a fair receipt of water,
of some thirty or forty foot square, but without fish,
or slime, or mud. For the first, the ornaments of
images gilt, or of marble, which are in use, do well :
but the main matter is, so to convey the water, as it
never stay, either in the bowls or in the cistern ; that
the water be never by rest discoloured, green or red
or the like, or gather any mossiness or putrefaction.
Besides that, it is to be cleansed every day by the
hand. Also some steps up to it, and some fine pavement about it, doth well. As for the other kind of
fountain, which we may call a bathing pool, it may
admit much curiosity and beauty, wherewith we will
not trouble ourselves : as, that the bottom be finely
paved, and with images ; the sides likewise ; and
withal embellished with coloured glass, and such
things of lustre ; encompassed also with fine rails of
low statuas. But the main point is the same which

we mentioned in the former kind of fountain ; which is, that the water be in perpetual motion, fed by a water higher than the pool, and delivered into it by fair spouts, and then discharged away under ground, by some equality of bores, that it stay little. And for fine devices, of arching water without spilling, and making it rise in several forms (of feathers, drinking glasses, canopies, and the like), they be pretty things to look on, but nothing to health and sweetness.

For the heath, which was the third part of our plot, I wish it to be framed, as much as may be, to a natural wildness. Trees I would have none in it ; but some thickets, made only of sweet-briar and honeysuckle, and some wild vine amongst ; and the ground set with violets, strawberries, and primroses. For these are sweet, and prosper in the shade. And these to be in the heath, here and there, not in any order. I like also little heaps, in the nature of mole-hills (such as are in wild heaths), to be set, some with wild thyme ; some with pinks ; some with ger-mander, that gives a good flower to the eye ; some with periwinkle ; some with violets ; some with strawberries ; some with cowslips ; some with daisies ; some with red roses ; some with lilium convallium ; some with sweet-williams red ; some with bear's-foot ; and the like low flowers, being withal sweet and sightly. Part of which heaps to be with standards of little bushes pricked upon their top, and part without. The standards to be roses ; juniper ; holly ; berberries (but here and there, be-cause of the smell of their blossom) ; red currants ; gooseberries ; rosemary ; bays ; sweet-briar ; and such like. But these standards to be kept with cutting, that they grow not out of course.

For the side grounds, you are to fill them with variety of alleys, private, to give a full shade, some of them, wheresoever the sun be. You are to frame some of them likewise for shelter, that when the wind blows sharp, you may walk as in a gallery. And those alleys must be likewise hedged at both ends, to keep out the wind ; and these closer alleys must be ever finely gravelled, and no grass, because of going wet. In many of these alleys likewise, you are to set fruit-trees of all sorts ; as well upon the walls as in ranges. And this would be generally observed, that the borders, wherein you plant your fruit-trees, be fair and large, and low, and not steep ; and set with fine flowers, but thin and sparingly, lest they deceive the trees. At the end of both the side grounds, I would have a mount of some pretty height, leaving the wall of the enclosure breast high, to look abroad into the fields.

For the main garden, I do not deny but there should be some fair alleys, ranged on both sides with fruit-trees ; and some pretty tufts of fruit-trees, and arbours with seats, set in some decent order ; but these to be by no means set too thick ; but to leave the main garden so as it be not close, but the air open and free. For as for shade, I would have you rest upon the alleys of the side grounds, there to walk, if you be disposed, in the heat of the year or day ; but to make account that the main garden is for the more temperate parts of the year ; and in the heat of summer, for the morning and the evening, or overcast days.

For aviaries, I like them not, except they be of that largeness as they may be turfed, and have living plants and bushes set in them ; that the birds may have more scope and natural nestling, and that no foulness appear in the floor of the aviary.

So I have made a platform of a princely garden, partly by precept, partly by drawing, not a model, but some general lines of it ; and in this I have spared

Deceive, Deprive.   *Platform*, Outline or plan.

for no cost. But it is nothing for great princes, that, for the most part, taking advice with workmen, with no less cost set their things together ; and sometimes add statuas, and such things, for state and magnificence, but nothing to the true pleasure of a garden.

ABRAHAM COWLEY

Of Greatness

SINCE we cannot attain to greatness, says the Sieur de
Montaigne, let us have our revenge by railing at it :
this he spoke but in jest.   I believe he desired it no
more than I do, and had less reason, for he enjoyed so
plentiful and honourable a fortune in a most excellent
country, as allowed him all the real conveniences of
it, separated and purged from the incommodities.   If
I were but in his condition, I should think it hard
measure, without being convinced of any crime, to be
sequestered from it and made one of the principal
officers of state.   But the reader may think that what
I now say is of small authority, because I never was,
nor ever shall be, put to the trial ; I can therefore
only make my protestation.

> If ever I more riches did desire
> Than cleanliness and quiet do require ;
> If e'er ambition did my fancy cheat,
> With any wish so mean as to be great,
> Continue, Heaven, still from me to remove
> The humble blessings of that life I love.

I know very many men will despise, and some pity
me, for this humour, as a poor-spirited fellow ; but I
am content, and, like Horace, thank God for being so.
*Dii bene fecerunt, inopis me quodque pusilli finxerunt
animi.*   I confess I love littleness almost in all things.
A little convenient estate, a little cheerful house, a
little company, and a very little feast ; and if I were

Dii bene, etc., The gods did well to make me of a poor and timid
spirit.

ever to fall in love again (which is a great passion, and therefore I hope I have done with it) it would be, I think, with prettiness rather than with majestical beauty. I would neither wish that my mistress, nor my fortune, should be a *bona roba*, nor, as Homer used to describe his beauties, like a daughter of great Jupiter, for the stateliness and largeness of her person, but, as Lucretius says, " *Parvula, pumilio, χαρίτων μία, tota merum sal.*"

Where there is one man of this, I believe there are a thousand of Senecio's mind, whose ridiculous affectation of grandeur Seneca the elder describes to this effect. Senecio was a man of a turbid and confused wit, who could not endure to speak any but mighty words and sentences, till this humour grew at last into so notorious a habit, or rather disease, as became the sport of the whole town : he would have no servants but huge massy fellows, no plate or household stuff but thrice as big as the fashion ; you may believe me, for I speak it without raillery, his extravagancy came at last into such a madness that he would not put on a pair of shoes each of which was not big enough for both his feet ; he would eat nothing but what was great, nor touch any fruit but horse-plums and pound-pears. He kept a concubine that was a very giantess, and made her walk, too, always in *chiopins*, till at last he got the surname of " *Senecio Grandio*," which, Messala said, was not his cognomen, but his cogno-mentum. When he declaimed for the three hundred Lacedæmonians, who also opposed Xerxes' army of above three hundred thousand, he stretched out his arms and stood on tiptoes, that he might appear the taller, and cried out in a very loud voice, " I rejoice, I rejoice ! " We wondered, I remember, what new great fortune had befallen his eminence. " Xerxes," says he, " is all mine own. He who took away the

Parvula, etc., Small and dwarfish, but one of the Graces, all pure wit. *Chiopins*, High shoes.

sight of the sea with the canvas veils of so many ships . . ." and then he goes on so, as I know not what to make of the rest, whether it be the fault of the edition, or the orator's own burly way of nonsense.

This is the character that Seneca gives of this hyperbolical fop, whom we stand amazed at, and yet there are very few men who are not, in some things, and to some degree, grandios. Is anything more common than to see our ladies of quality wear such high shoes as they cannot walk in without one to lead them ? and a gown as long again as their body, so that they cannot stir to the next room without a page or two to hold it up ? I may safely say that all the ostentation of our grandees is just like a train, of no use in the world, but horribly cumbersome and incommodious. What is all this but spice of *grandio !* How tedious would this be if we were always bound to it ! I do believe there is no king who would not rather be deposed than endure every day of his reign all the ceremonies of his coronation. The mightiest princes are glad to fly often from these majestic pleasures (which is, methinks, no small disparagement to them), as it were for refuge, to the most contemptible divertisements and meanest recreations of the vulgar, nay, even of children. One of the most powerful and fortunate princes of the world of late could find out no delight so satisfactory as the keeping of little singing-birds, and hearing of them and whistling to them. What did the emperors of the whole world ? If ever any men had the free and full enjoyment of all human greatness (nay, that would not suffice, for they would be gods too) they certainly possessed it ; and yet one of them, who styled himself " Lord and God of the Earth," could not tell how to pass his whole day pleasantly, without spending constant two or three hours in catching of flies, and killing them with a bodkin, as if his godship had been Beelzebub. One of his predecessors, Nero (who never put any bounds, nor met with any stop to his appetite), could divert himself with no pastime more agreeable than to run about the streets all night in a disguise, and abuse the women and affront the men whom he met, and sometimes to beat them, and sometimes to be beaten by them. This was one of his imperial nocturnal pleasures ; his chiefest in the day was to sing and play upon a fiddle, in the habit of a minstrel, upon the public stage ; he was prouder of the garlands that were given to his divine voice (as they called it then) in those kind of prizes, than all his forefathers were of their triumphs over nations. He did not at his death complain that so mighty an emperor, and the last of all the Cæsarian race of deities, should be brought to so shameful and miserable an end, but only cried out, " Alas ! what pity it is that so excellent a musician should perish in this manner ! " His uncle Claudius spent half his time at playing at dice ; that was the main fruit of his sovereignty. I omit the madnesses of Caligula's delights, and the execrable sordidness of those of Tiberius. Would one think that Augustus himself, the highest and most fortunate of mankind, a person endowed too with many excellent parts of nature, should be so hard put to it sometimes for want of recreations, as to be found playing at nuts and bounding-stones with little Syrian and Moorish boys, whose company he took delight in for their prating and their wantonness ?

Was it for this, that Rome's best blood he spilt,
With so much falsehood, so much guilt ?
Was it for this that his ambition strove
To equal Cæsar first, and after Jove ?
Greatness is barren sure of solid joys ;
Her merchandise, I fear, is all in toys ;
She could not else sure so uncivil be,
To treat his universal majesty,
His new created Deity,
With nuts and bounding-stones and boys.

But we must excuse her for this meagre entertainment ; she has not really wherewithal to make such feasts as we imagine ; her guests must be contented sometimes with but slender cates, and with the same cold meats served over and over again, even till they become nauseous. When you have pared away all the vanity, what solid and natural contentment does there remain which may not be had with five hundred pounds a year ? Not so many servants or horses, but a few good ones, which will do all the business as well ; not so many choice dishes at every meal, but at several meals all of them, which makes them both the more healthy and the more pleasant ; not so rich garments nor so frequent changes, but as warm and as comely, and so frequent change, too, as is every jot as good for the master, though not for the tailor or valet-de-chambre ; not such a stately palace, nor gilt rooms, nor the costlier sorts of tapestry, but a convenient brick house, with decent wainscot and pretty forest-work hangings. Lastly (for I omit all other particulars, and will end with that which I love most in both conditions), not whole woods cut in walks, nor vast parks, nor fountain or cascade gardens, but herb and flower and fruit gardens, which are more useful, and the water every whit as clear and wholesome as if it darted from the breasts of a marble nymph or the urn of a river-god. If for all this you like better the substance of that former estate of life, do but consider the inseparable accidents of both : servitude, disquiet, danger, and most commonly guilt, inherent in the one ; in the other, liberty, tranquillity, security, and innocence : and when you have thought upon this, you will confess that to be a truth which appeared to you before but a ridiculous paradox, that a low fortune is better guarded and attended than a high one. If, indeed, we look only upon the flourishing head of the tree, it appears a most beautiful object.

—— *Sed quantum vertice ad auras*
Ætherias, tantum radice ad Tartara tendit.

As far up towards heaven the branches grow,
So far the root sinks down to hell below.

Another horrible disgrace to greatness is, that it is
for the most part in pitiful want and distress. What
a wonderful thing is this, unless it degenerate into
avarice, and so cease to be greatness. It falls perpetually into such necessities as drive it into all the
meanest and most sordid ways of borrowing, cozenage,
and robbery, *Mancipiis locuples, eget aeris Cappa-*
docum Rex. This is the case of almost all great men,
as well as of the poor king of Cappadocia. They
abound with slaves, but are indigent of money. The
ancient Roman emperors, who had the riches of the
whole world for their revenue, had wherewithal to
live, one would have thought, pretty well at ease, and
to have been exempt from the pressures of extreme
poverty. But yet with most of them it was much
otherwise, and they fell perpetually into such miserable penury, that they were forced to devour or
squeeze most of their friends and servants, to cheat
with infamous projects, to ransack and pillage all
their provinces. This fashion of imperial grandeur is
imitated by all inferior and subordinate sorts of it,
as if it were a point of honour. They must be cheated
of a third part of their estates, two other thirds they
must expend in vanity, so that they remain debtors
for all the necessary provisions of life, and have no
way to satisfy those debts but out of the succours and
supplies of rapine ; " as riches increase," says Solo-
mon, " so do the mouths that devour it." The master
mouth has no more than before ; the owner, methinks,
is like Ocnus in the fable, who is perpetually winding
a rope of hay and an ass at the end perpetually eating
it. Out of these inconveniences arises naturally one
more, which is, that no greatness can be satisfied or

contented with itself : still, if it could mount up a
little higher, it would be happy ; if it could but gain
that point, it would obtain all its desires ; but yet at
last, when it is got up to the very top of the peak of
Teneriffe, it is in very great danger of breaking its
neck downwards, but in no possibility of ascending
upwards into the seat of tranquillity above the moon.
The first ambitious men in the world, the old giants,
are said to have made an heroical attempt of scaling
Heaven in despite of the gods, and they cast Ossa
upon Olympus and Pelion upon Ossa, two or three
mountains more they thought would have done their
business, but the thunder spoiled all the work when
they were come up to the third storey ;

> And what a noble plot was crossed,
> And what a brave design was lost.

A famous person of their offspring, the late giant of
our nation, when, from the condition of a very inconsiderable captain, he had made himself lieutenant-
general of an army of little Titans, which was his first
mountain ; and afterwards general, which was his
second ; and after that absolute tyrant of three kingdoms, which was the third, and almost touched the
heaven which he affected ; is believed to have died
with grief and discontent because he could not attain
to the honest name of a king, and the old formality of
a crown, though he had before exceeded the power by
a wicked usurpation. If he could have compassed
that, he would perhaps have wanted something else
that is necessary to felicity, and pined away for the
want of the title of an emperor or a god. The reason
of this is, that greatness has no reality in nature, but
is a creature of the fancy—a notion that consists only
in relation and comparison. It is indeed an idol ;
but St. Paul teaches us that an idol is nothing in the
world. There is in truth no rising or meridian of the

sun, but only in respect to several places : there is no right or left, no upper hand in nature ; everything is little and everything is great according as it is diversely compared. There may be perhaps some villages in Scotland or Ireland where I might be a great man ; and in that case I should be like Cæsar—you would wonder how Cæsar and I should be like one another in anything—and choose rather to be the first man of the village than second at Rome. Our country is called Great Britain, in regard only of a lesser of the same name ; it would be but a ridiculous epithet for it when we consider it together with the kingdom of China. That, too, is but a pitiful rood of ground in comparison of the whole earth besides ; and this whole globe of earth, which we account so immense a body, is but one point or atom in relation to those numberless worlds that are scattered up and down in the infinite space of the sky which we behold. The other many inconveniences of grandeur I have spoken of dispersedly in several chapters, and shall end this with an ode of Horace, not exactly copied but rudely imitated.

HORACE, LIB. 3, ODE 1

Odi profanum vulgus, etc.

I

Hence, ye profane ; I hate ye all ;
Both the great vulgar, and the small.
To virgin minds, which yet their native whiteness
    hold,
Not yet discoloured with the love of gold
      (That jaundice of the soul,
Which makes it look so gilded and so foul),
To you, ye very few, these truths I tell ;
The muse inspires my song, hark, and observe it well.

II

We look on men, and wonder at such odds
    'Twixt things that were the same by birth ;
We look on kings as giants of the earth,
These giants are but pigmies to the gods.
    The humblest bush and proudest oak
Are but of equal proof against the thunder-stroke.
Beauty and strength, and wit, and wealth, and power
    Have their short flourishing hour,
    And love to see themselves, and smile,
And joy in their pre-eminence a while ;
    Even so in the same land,
Poor weeds, rich corn, gay flowers together stand ;
Alas, death mows down all with an impartial hand.

III

And all you men, whom greatness does so please,
    Ye feast, I fear, like Damocles.
    If you your eyes could upwards move,
(But you, I fear, think nothing is above)
You would perceive by what a little thread
    The sword still hangs over your head.
No tide of wine would drown your cares,
No mirth or music over-noise your fears ;
The fear of death would you so watchful keep,
As not to admit the image of it, sleep.

IV

Sleep is a god too proud to wait in palaces ;
And yet so humble, too, as not to scorn
    The meanest country cottages ;
    His poppy grows among the corn.
The halcyon sleep will never build his nest
    In any stormy breast.

'Tis not enough that he does find
    Clouds and darkness in their mind ;
Darkness but half his work will do,
'Tis not enough ; he must find quiet too.

V

The man who, in all wishes he does make,
    Does only Nature's counsel take,
That wise and happy man will never fear
    The evil aspects of the year,
Nor tremble, though two comets should appear.
He does not look in almanacks to see
    Whether he fortunate shall be ;
Let Mars and Saturn in the heavens conjoin,
And what they please against the world design,
    So Jupiter within him shine.

VI

If of their pleasures and desires no end be found ;
God to their cares and fears will set no bound.
    What would content you ?   Who can tell ?
Ye fear so much to lose what you have got
    As if ye liked it well.
Ye strive for more, as if ye liked it not.
    Go, level hills, and fill up seas,
Spare nought that may your wanton fancy please ;
    But trust me, when you have done all this,
Much will be missing still, and much will be amiss.

Of Myself

IT is a hard and nice subject for a man to write of
himself ; it grates his own heart to say anything of
disparagement and the reader's ears to hear anything

of praise for him. There is no danger from me of offending him in this kind ; neither my mind, nor my body, nor my fortune allow me any materials for that vanity. It is sufficient for my own contentment that they have preserved me from being scandalous, or remarkable on the defective side. But besides that, I shall here speak of myself only in relation to the subject of these precedent discourses, and shall be likelier thereby to fall into the contempt than rise up to the estimation of most people. As far as my memory can return back into my past life, before I knew or was capable of guessing what the world, or glories, or business of it were, the natural affections of my soul gave me a secret bent of aversion from them, as some plants are said to turn away from others by an antipathy imperceptible to themselves and inscrutable to man's understanding. Even when I was a very young boy at school, instead of running about on holidays and playing with my fellows, I was wont to steal from them and walk into the fields, either alone with a book, or with some one companion, if I could find any of the same temper. I was then, too, so much an enemy to all constraint, that my masters could never prevail on me, by any persuasions or encouragements, to learn without book the common rules of grammar, in which they dispensed with me alone, because they found I made a shift to do the usual exercises out of my own reading and observation. That I was then of the same mind as I am now (which I confess I wonder at myself) may appear by the latter end of an ode which I made when I was but thirteen years old, and which was then printed with many other verses. The beginning of it is boyish, but of this part which I here set down, if a very little were corrected, I should hardly now be much ashamed.

IX

This only grant me, that my means may lie
Too low for envy, for contempt too high.
    Some honour I would have,
Not from great deeds, but good alone.
The unknown are better than ill known.
    Rumour can ope the grave ;
Acquaintance I would have, but when it depends
Not on the number, but the choice of friends.

X

Books should, not business, entertain the light,
And sleep, as undisturbed as death, the night.
    My house a cottage, more
Than palace, and should fitting be
For all my use, no luxury.
    My garden painted o'er
With Nature's hand, not Art's ; and pleasures yield,
Horace might envy in his Sabine field.

XI

Thus would I double my life's fading space,
For he that runs it well twice runs his race.
    And in this true delight,
These unbought sports, this happy state,
I would not fear, nor wish my fate,
    But boldly say each night,
To-morrow let my sun his beams display
Or in clouds hide them—I have lived to-day.

You may see by it I was even then acquainted with
the poets (for the conclusion is taken out of Horace),
and perhaps it was the immature and immoderate love
of them which stamped first, or rather engraved, these

characters in me. They were like letters cut into the
bark of a young tree, which with the tree still grow
proportionably. But how this love came to be produced in me so early is a hard question. I believe I
can tell the particular little chance that filled my head
first with such chimes of verse as have never since left
ringing there. For I remember when I began to read,
and to take some pleasure in it, there was wont to lie
in my mother's parlour (I know not by what accident,
for she herself never in her life read any book but of
devotion), but there was wont to lie Spenser's works ;
this I happened to fall upon, and was infinitely delighted with the stories of the knights, and giants,
and monsters, and brave houses, which I found everywhere there (though my understanding had little to
do with all this) ; and by degrees with the tinkling of
the rhyme and dance of the numbers, so that I think
I had read him all over before I was twelve years old,
and was thus made a poet immediately. . . .

With these affections of mind, and my heart wholly
set upon letters, I went to the university, but was
soon torn from thence by that violent public storm
which would suffer nothing to stand where it did,
but rooted up every plant, even from the princely
cedars to me, the hyssop. Yet I had as good fortune as could have befallen me in such a tempest ;
for I was cast by it into the family of one of the
best persons, and into the court of one of the best
princesses of the world. Now though I was here engaged in ways most contrary to the original design
of my life, that is, into much company, and no small
business, and into a daily sight of greatness, both
militant and triumphant, for that was the state then
of the English and French Courts ; yet all this was so
far from altering my opinion, that it only added the
confirmation of reason to that which was before but
natural inclination. I saw plainly all the paint of that
kind of life, the nearer I came to it ; and that beauty

which I did not fall in love with when, for aught I knew, it was real, was not like to bewitch or entice me when I saw that it was adulterate. I met with several great persons, whom I liked very well, but could not perceive that any part of their greatness was to be liked or desired, no more than I would be glad or content to be in a storm, though I saw many ships which rode safely and bravely in it. A storm would not agree with my stomach, if it did my with courage. Though I was in a crowd of as good company as could be found anywhere, though I was in business of great and honourable trust, though I ate at the best table, and enjoyed the best conveniences for present subsistence that ought to be desired by a man of my condition in banishment and public distresses, yet I could not abstain from renewing my old schoolboy's wish in a copy of verses to the same effect.

> Well then ; I now do plainly see,
> This busy world and I shall ne'er agree, etc.

And I never then proposed to myself any other advantage from his Majesty's happy restoration, but the getting into some moderately convenient retreat in the country, which I thought in that case I might easily have compassed, as well as some others, with no greater probabilities or pretences, have arrived to extraordinary fortunes. But I had before written a shrewd prophecy against myself, and I think Apollo inspired me in the truth, though not in the elegance of it.

> Thou, neither great at court nor in the war,
> Nor at th' exchange shalt be, nor at the wrangling bar ;
> Content thyself with the small barren praise,
> Which neglected verse does raise, etc.

However, by the failing of the forces which I had expected, I did not quit the design which I had resolved on ; I cast myself into it *A corps perdu*, without making capitulations or taking counsel of fortune. But God laughs at a man who says to his soul, " Take thy ease " : I met presently not only with many little encumbrances and impediments, but with so much sickness (a new misfortune to me) as would have spoiled the happiness of an emperor as well as mine. Yet I do neither repent nor alter my course. *Non ego perfidum dixi sacramentum.* Nothing shall separate me from a mistress which I have loved so long, and have now at last married, though she neither has brought me a rich portion, nor lived yet so quietly with me as I hoped from her.

———— *Nec vos, dulcissima mundi*
Nomina, vos Musæ, libertas, otia, libri,
Hortique sylvæque anima remanente relinquam.

Nor by me e'er shall you,
You of all names the sweetest, and the best,
You Muses, books, and liberty, and rest ;
You gardens, fields, and woods forsaken be,
As long as life itself forsakes not me.

But this is a very pretty ejaculation. Because I have concluded all the other chapters with a copy of verses, I will maintain the humour to the last.

MARTIAL, LIB. 10, EP. 47

Vitam quæ faciunt beatiorem, etc.

Since, dearest friend, 'tis your desire to see
A true receipt of happiness from me ;
These are the chief ingredients, if not all :
Take an estate neither too great nor small,
Which *quantum sufficit* the doctors call ;
Let this estate from parents' care descend :
The getting it too much of life does spend.

Take such a ground, whose gratitude may be
A fair encouragement for industry.
Let constant fires the winter's fury tame,
And let thy kitchens be a vestal flame.
Thee to the town let never suit at law,
And rarely, very rarely, business draw.
Thy active mind in equal temper keep,
In undisturbèd peace, yet not in sleep.
Let exercise a vigorous health maintain,
Without which all the composition's vain.
In the same weight prudence and innocence take ;
Ana of each does the just mixture make.
But a few friendships wear, and let them be
By nature and by Fortune fit for thee.
Instead of art and luxury in food,
Let mirth and freedom make thy table good.
If any cares into thy daytime creep,
At night, without wines, opium, let them sleep.
Let rest, which Nature does to darkness wed,
And not lust, recommend to thee thy bed,
Be satisfied, and pleased with what thou art ;
Act cheerfully and well the allotted part.
Enjoy the present hour, be thankful for the past,
And neither fear, nor wish the approaches of the last.

MARTIAL, LIB. 10, EP. 96

Me, who have lived so long among the great,
You wonder to hear talk of a retreat :
And a retreat so distant, as may show
No thoughts of a return when once I go.
Give me a country, how remote so e'er,
Where happiness a moderate rate does bear,
Where poverty itself in plenty flows
And all the solid use of riches knows.
The ground about the house maintains it there,
The house maintains the ground about it here.

Here even hunger's dear, and a full board
Devours the vital substance of the lord.
The land itself does there the feast bestow,
The land itself must here to market go.
Three or four suits one winter here does waste,
One suit does there three or four winters last.
Here every frugal man must oft be cold,
And little lukewarm fires are to you sold.
There fire's an element as cheap and free
Almost as any of the other three.
Stay you then here, and live among the great,
Attend their sports, and at their tables eat.
When all the bounties here of men you score:
The Place's bounty there, shall give me more.

RICHARD STEELE

Recollections of Childhood

Dies, ni fallor, adest, quem semper acerbum,
Semper honoratum, sic dii voluistis, habebo.
VIRG., *Æn.* v. 49.

THERE are those among mankind, who can enjoy no relish of their being, except the world is made acquainted with all that relates to them, and think every thing lost that passes unobserved ; but others find a solid delight in stealing by the crowd, and modelling their life after such a manner, as is as much above the approbation as the practice of the vulgar. Life being too short to give instances great enough of true friendship or good will, some sages have thought it pious to preserve a certain reverence for the names of their deceased friends ; and have withdrawn themselves from the rest of the world at certain seasons, to commemorate in their own thoughts such of their acquaintance who have gone before them out of this life. And indeed, when we are advanced in years, there is not a more pleasing entertainment, than to recollect in a gloomy moment the many we have parted with, that have been dear and agreeable to us, and to cast a melancholy thought or two after those, with whom, perhaps, we have indulged ourselves in whole nights of mirth and jollity. With such inclinations in my heart I went to my closet yesterday in the evening, and resolved to be sorrowful ; upon which occasion I could not but look with disdain upon myself, that though all the reasons which I had to lament the loss of many of my friends are now as forcible as at the moment of their departure, yet did not my heart swell with the same sorrow which I felt at the time ; but I could, without tears, reflect upon many pleasing adventures I have had with some, who have long been blended with common earth. Though it is by the benefit of nature, that length of time thus blots out the violence of afflictions ; yet, with tempers too much given to pleasure, it is almost necessary to revive the old places of grief in our memory ; and ponder step by step on past life, to lead the mind into that sobriety of thought which poises the heart, and makes it beat with due time, without being quickened with desire, or retarded with despair, from its proper and equal motion. When we wind up a clock that is out of order, to make it go well for the future, we do not immediately set the hand to the present instant, but we make it strike the round of all its hours, before it can recover the regularity of its time. Such, thought I, shall be my method this evening ; and since it is that day of the year which I dedicate to the memory of such in another life as I much delighted in when living, an hour or two shall be sacred to sorrow and their memory, while I run over all the melancholy circumstances of this kind which have occurred to me in my whole life.

The first sense of sorrow I ever knew was upon the death of my father, at which time I was not quite five years of age ; but was rather amazed at what all the house meant, than possessed with a real understanding why nobody was willing to play with me. I remember I went into the room where his body lay, and my mother sat weeping alone by it. I had my battledore in my hand, and fell a-beating the coffin, and calling Papa ; for, I know not how, I had some slight idea that he was locked up there. My mother caught me in her arms, and, transported beyond all patience of the silent grief she was before in, she almost smothered me in her embraces ; and told me in a flood of tears, Papa could not hear me, and would play with me no more, for they were going to put him under ground, whence he could never come to us again. She was a very beautiful woman, of a noble spirit, and there was a dignity in her grief amidst all the wildness of her transport, which, methought, struck me with an instinct of sorrow, that, before I was sensible of what it was to grieve, seized my very soul, and has made pity the weakness of my heart ever since. The mind in infancy is, methinks, like the body in embryo ; and receives impressions so forcible, that they are as hard to be removed by reason, as any mark with which a child is born is to be taken away by any future application. Hence it is, that good nature in me is no merit ; but having been so frequently overwhelmed with her tears before I knew the cause of any affliction, or could draw defences from my own judgment, I imbibed commiseration, remorse, and an unmanly gentleness of mind, which has since insnared me into ten thousand calamities ; and from whence I can reap no advantage, except it be, that, in such a humour as I am now in, I can the better indulge myself in the softnesses of humanity, and enjoy that sweet anxiety which arises from the memory of past afflictions.

We, that are very old, are better able to remember things which befell us in our distant youth, than the passages of later days. For this reason it is, that the companions of my strong and vigorous years present themselves more immediately to me in this office of sorrow. Untimely and unhappy deaths are what we are most apt to lament ; so little are we able to make it indifferent when a thing happens, though we know it must happen. Thus we groan under life, and bewail those who are relieved from it. Every object that returns to our imagination raises different passions, according to the circumstance of their departure. Who can have lived in an army, and in a serious hour reflect upon the many gay and agreeable men that might long have flourished in the arts of peace, and not join with the imprecations of the fatherless and widows on the tyrant to whose ambition they fell sacrifices ? But gallant men, who are cut off by the sword, move rather our veneration than our pity ; and we gather relief enough from their own contempt of death, to make that no evil, which was approached with so much cheerfulness, and attended with so much honour. But when we turn our thoughts from the great parts of life on such occasions, and instead of lamenting those who stood ready to give death to those from whom they had the fortune to receive it ; I say, when we let our thoughts wander from such noble objects, and consider the havoc which is made among the tender and the innocent, pity enters with an unmixed softness, and possesses all our souls at once.

Here (were there words to express such sentiments with proper tenderness) I should record the beauty, innocence, and untimely death, of the first object my eyes ever beheld with love. The beauteous virgin ! how ignorantly did she charm, how carelessly excel ? Oh death ! thou hast right to the bold, to the ambitious, to the high, and to the haughty ; but why this cruelty to the humble, to the meek, to the undiscerning, to the thoughtless ? Nor age, nor business, nor distress, can erase the dear image from my imagination. In the same week I saw her dressed for a ball, and in a shroud. How ill did the habit of death become the pretty trifler ? I still behold the smiling earth——A large train of disasters were coming on to my memory, when my servant knocked at my closet-door, and interrupted me with a letter, attended with a hamper of wine, of the same sort with that which is to be put to sale on Thursday next, at Garraway's coffee-house. Upon the receipt of it, I sent for three of my friends.　We are so intimate, that we can be company in whatever state of mind we meet, and can entertain each other without expecting always to rejoice.　The wine we found to be generous and warming, but with such a heat as moved us rather to be cheerful than frolicsome.　It revived the spirits, without firing the blood.　We commended it until two of the clock this morning ; and having to-day met a little before dinner, we found, that though we drank two bottles a man, we had much more reason to recollect than forget what had passed the night before.

A Day in London

Sine me, vacivum tempus ne quod dem mihı
Laboris.—TER., *Heaut.*, Act I. Sc. i.

IT is an inexpressible pleasure to know a little of the world, and be of no character or significancy in it.

To be ever unconcerned, and ever looking on new objects with an endless curiosity, is a delight known only to those who are turned for speculation : nay, they who enjoy it must value things only as they are the objects of speculation, without drawing any worldly advantage to themselves from them, but just as they are what contribute to their amusement, or the improvement of the mind.　I lay one night last week at Richmond ; and being restless, not out of dissatisfaction, but a certain busy inclination one sometimes has, I rose at four in the morning, and took boat for London, with a resolution to rove by boat and coach for the next four-and-twenty hours, till the many different objects I must needs meet with should tire my imagination, and give me an inclination to a repose more profound than I was at that time capable of.　I beg people's pardon for an odd humour I am guilty of, and was often that day, which is saluting any person whom I like, whether I know him or not. This is a particularity would be tolerated in me, if they considered that the greatest pleasure I know I receive at my eyes, and that I am obliged to an agreeable person for coming abroad into my view, as another is for a visit of conversation at their own houses.

The hours of the day and night are taken up in the cities of London and Westminster, by people as different from each other as those who are born in different centuries. Men of six o'clock give way to those of nine, they of nine to the generation of twelve; and they of twelve disappear, and make room for the fashionable world, who have made two o'clock the noon of the day.

When we first put off from shore, we soon fell in with a fleet of gardeners, bound for the several market ports of London; and it was the most pleasing scene imaginable to see the cheerfulness with which those industrious people plied their way to a certain sale of their goods. The banks on each side are as well peopled, and beautified with as agreeable plantations, as any spot on the earth; but the Thames itself, loaded with the product of each shore, added very much to the landscape. It was very easy to observe by their sailing, and the countenances of the ruddy virgins, who were supercargoes, the parts of the town to which they were bound. There was an air in the purveyors for Covent-garden, who frequently converse with morning rakes, very unlike the seeming sobriety of those bound for Stocks-market.

Nothing remarkable happened in our voyage; but I landed with ten sail of apricot-boats, at Strand-bridge, after having put in at Nine-Elms, and taken in melons, consigned by Mr. Cuffe, of that place, to Sarah Sewell and Company, at their stall in Covent-garden. We arrived at Strand-bridge at six of the clock, and were unloading; when the hackney-coach-

men of the foregoing night took their leave of each
other at the Dark-house, to go to bed before the day
was too far spent. Chimney-sweepers passed by us as
we made up to the market, and some raillery happened
between one of the fruit-wenches and those black men
about the Devil and Eve, with allusion to their several
professions. I could not believe any place more entertaining than Covent-garden ; where I strolled from
one fruit-shop to another, with crowds of agreeable
young women around me, who were purchasing fruit
for their respective families. It was almost eight of
the clock before I could leave that variety of objects.
I took coach and followed a young lady, who tripped
into another just before me, attended by her maid.
I saw immediately she was of the family of the Vain-
loves. There are a set of these, who, of all things,
affect the play of Blind-man's-buff, and leading men
into love for they know not whom, who are fled they
know not where. This sort of woman is usually a
jaunty slattern ; she hangs on her clothes, plays her
head, varies her posture, and changes place incessantly,
and all with an appearance of striving at the same
time to hide herself, and yet give you to understand
she is in humour to laugh at you. You must have
often seen the coachmen make signs with their fingers,
as they drive by each other, to intimate how much
they have got that day. They can carry on that
language to give intelligence where they are driving.
In an instant my coachman took the wink to pursue ;
and the lady's driver gave the hint that he was going
through Long-acre towards St. James's ; while he
whipped up James-street, we drove for King-street, to
save the pass at St. Martin's-lane. The coachmen
took care to meet, jostle, and threaten each other for
way, and be entangled at the end of Newport-street
and Long-acre. The fright, you must believe, brought
down the lady's coach-door, and obliged her, with her
mask off, to inquire into the bustle,—when she sees

the man she would avoid. The tackle of the coach-window is so bad she cannot draw it up again, and she drives on sometimes wholly discovered, and sometimes half-escaped, according to the accident of carriages in her way. One of these ladies keeps her seat in a hackney-coach, as well as the best rider does on a managed horse. The laced shoe on her left foot, with a careless gesture, just appearing on the opposite cushion, held her both firm, and in a proper attitude to receive the next jolt.

As she was an excellent coach-woman, many were the glances at each other which we had for an hour and a half, in all parts of the town, by the skill of our drivers ; till at last my lady was conveniently lost, with notice from her coachman to ours to make off, and he should hear where she went. This chase was now at an end : and the fellow who drove her came to us, and discovered that he was ordered to come again in an hour, for that she was a silk-worm. I was surprised with this phrase, but found it was a cant among the hackney fraternity for their best customers, women who ramble twice or thrice a week from shop to shop, to turn over all the goods in town without buying anything. The silk-worms are, it seems, indulged by the tradesmen ; for, though they never buy, they are ever talking of new silks, laces, and ribbons, and serve the owners in getting them customers, as their common dunners do in making them pay.

The day of people of fashion began now to break, and carts and hacks were mingled with equipages of show and vanity ; when I resolved to walk it out of cheapness ; but my unhappy curiosity is such, that I find it always my interest to take coach ; for some odd adventure among beggars, ballad-singers, or the like, detains and throws me into expense. It happened so immediately : for at the corner of Warwick-street, as I was listening to a new ballad, a ragged rascal, a beggar who knew me, came up to me, and began to turn the eyes of the good company upon me, by telling me he was extremely poor, and should die in the street for want of drink, except I immediately would have the charity to give him sixpence to go into the next ale-house and save his life. He urged, with a melancholy face, that all his family had died of thirst. All the mob have humour, and two or three began to take the jest ; by which Mr. Sturdy carried his point, and let me sneak off to a coach. As I drove along, it was a pleasing reflection to see the world so prettily checkered since I left Richmond, and the scene still filling with children of a new hour. This satisfaction increased as I moved towards the city ; and gay signs, well-disposed streets, magnificent public structures, and wealthy shops adorned with contented faces, made the joy still rising till we came into the centre of the city, and centre of the world of trade, the Exchange of London. As other men in the crowds about me were pleased with their hopes and bargains, I found my account in observing them, in attention to their several interests. I, indeed, looked upon myself as the richest man that walked the Exchange that day ; for my benevolence made me share the gains of every bargain that was made. It was not the least of my satisfaction in my survey, to go upstairs, and pass the shops of agreeable females ; to observe so many pretty hands busy in the folding of ribbons, and the utmost eagerness of agreeable faces in the sale of patches, pins, and wires, on each side of the counters, was an amusement in which I could longer have indulged myself, had not the dear creatures called to me, to ask what I wanted, when I could not answer, only " To look at you." I went to one of the windows which opened to the area below, where all the several voices lost their distinction, and rose up in a confused humming ; which created in me a reflection that could not come into the mind of any but of one a little too studious ; for I said to myself with a kind of pun in thought, " What nonsense is all the hurry of this world to those who are above it ? " In these, or not much wiser thoughts, I had like to have lost my place at the chop-house, where every man, according to the natural bashfulness or sullenness of our nation, eats in a public room a mess of broth, or chop of meat, in dumb silence, as if they had no pretence to speak to each other on the foot of being men, except they were of each other's acquaintance.

I went afterward to Robin's, and saw people, who had dined with me at the five-penny ordinary just before, give bills for the value of large estates ; and could not but behold with great pleasure, property lodged in, and transferred in a moment from, such as would never be masters of half as much as is seemingly in them, and given from them, every day they live. But before five in the afternoon I left the city, came to my common scene of Covent-garden, and passed the evening at Will's in attending the discourses of several sets of people, who relieved each other within my hearing on the subjects of cards, dice, love, learning, and politics. The last subject kept me till I heard the streets in the possession of the bellman, who had now the world to himself, and cried, " Past two o'clock." This roused me from my seat ; and I went to my lodgings, led by a light, whom I put into the discourse of his private economy, and made him give me an account of the charge, hazard, profit, and loss of a family that depended upon a link, with a design to end my trivial day with the generosity of sixpence, instead of a third part of that sum. When I came to my chambers, I writ down these minutes ; but was at a loss what instruction I should propose to my reader from the enumeration of so many insignificant matters and occurrences ; and I thought it of great use, if they could learn with me to keep their minds open to gratification, and ready to receive it from anything it meets with. This one circumstance will make every face you see give you the satisfaction you now take in beholding that of a friend ; will make every object a pleasing one ; will make all the good which arrives to any man, an increase of happiness to yourself.

JOSEPH ADDISON

The Tombs in Westminster Abbey

Pallida mors æquo pulsat pede pauperum tabernas
  Regumque turres, o beate Sexti.
Vitæ summa brevis spem nos vetat inchoare longam.
  Jam te premet nox, fabulæque manes,
Et domus exilis Plutonia——

Hor., 1 Od. iv. 13.

WHEN I am in a serious humour, I very often walk by myself in Westminster Abbey ; where the gloominess of the place, and the use to which it is applied, with the solemnity of the building, and the condition of the people who lie in it, are apt to fill the mind with a kind of melancholy, or rather thoughtfulness, that is not disagreeable. I yesterday passed a whole afternoon in the churchyard, the cloisters, and the church, amusing myself with the tombstones and inscriptions that I met with in those several regions of the dead. Most of them recorded nothing else of the buried person but that he was born upon one day and died upon another : the whole history of his life being comprehended in those two circumstances that are common to all mankind. I could not but look upon these registers of existence, whether of brass or marble, as a kind of satire upon the departed persons ; who had left no other memorial of them, but that they were born and that they died. They put me in mind of several persons mentioned in the battles of heroic poems, who have sounding names given them for no other reason but that they may be killed, and are celebrated for nothing but being knocked on the head.

Τλαῦκόν τε Μέδοντα τε Θερσιλοχόν τε.—Hom.

Glaucumque, Medontaque, Thersilochumque.—Vir.

The life of these men is finely described in Holy Writ by the path of an arrow, which is immediately closed up and lost.

Upon my going into the church, I entertained myself with the digging of a grave ; and saw in every shovel-ful of it that was thrown up, the fragment of a bone or skull intermixed with a kind of fresh mouldering earth that some time or other had a place in the composition of a human body. Upon this I began to consider with myself what innumerable multitudes of people lay con-fused together under the pavement of that ancient cathedral ; how men and women, friends and enemies, priests and soldiers, monks and prebendaries, were crumbled amongst one another, and blended together in the same common mass ; how beauty, strength, and youth, with old age, weakness, and deformity, lay undistinguished in the same promiscuous heap of matter.

After having thus surveyed this great magazine of mortality, as it were in the lump, I examined it more particularly by the accounts which I found on several of the monuments which are raised in every quarter of that ancient fabric. Some of them were covered with such extravagant epitaphs that, if it were possible for the dead person to be acquainted with them, he would blush at the praises which his friends have bestowed upon him. There are others so excessively modest that they deliver the character of the person departed in Greek or Hebrew, and by that means are not understood once in a twelvemonth. In the poetical quarter, I found there were poets who had no monuments, and monuments which had no poets. I observed indeed that the present war had filled the church with many of these uninhabited monuments, which had been erected to the memory of persons whose bodies were perhaps buried in the plains of Blenheim, or in the bosom of the ocean.

I could not but be very much delighted with several modern epitaphs, which are written with great elegance of expression and justness of thought, and therefore do honour to the living as well as to the dead. As a foreigner is very apt to conceive an idea of the ignorance or politeness of a nation from the turn of their public monuments and inscriptions, they should be submitted to the perusal of men of learning and genius before they are put in execution. Sir Cloudesly Shovel's monument has very often given me great offence. Instead of the brave, rough English admiral, which was the distinguishing character of that plain, gallant man, he is represented on his tomb by the figure of a beau, dressed in a long periwig, and reposing himself upon velvet cushions under a canopy of state. The inscription is answerable to the monument; for instead of celebrating the many remarkable actions he had performed in the service of his country, it acquaints us only with the manner of his death, in which it was impossible for him to reap any honour. The Dutch, whom we are apt to despise for want of genius, show an infinitely greater taste of antiquity and politeness in their buildings and works of this nature, than what we meet with in those of our own country. The monuments of their admirals, which have been erected at the public expense, represent them like themselves, and are adorned with rostral crowns and naval ornaments, with beautiful festoons of seaweed, shells, and coral.

But to return to our subject. I have left the repository of our English kings for the contemplation of another day, when I shall find my mind disposed for so serious an amusement. I know that entertain-

ments of this nature are apt to raise dark and dismal
thoughts in timorous minds and gloomy imaginations;
but for my own part, though I am always serious, I do
not know what it is to be melancholy, and can therefore take a view of nature in her deep and solemn
scenes, with the same pleasure as in her most gay and
delightful ones. By this means, I can improve myself
with those objects which others consider with terror.
When I look upon the tombs of the great, every emotion of envy dies in me; when I read the epitaphs of
the beautiful, every inordinate desire goes out; when
I meet with the grief of parents upon a tombstone,
my heart melts with compassion; when I see the
tomb of the parents themselves, I consider the vanity
of grieving for those whom we must quickly follow;
when I see kings lying by those who deposed them,
when I consider rival wits placed side by side, or the
holy men that divided the world with their contests
and disputes, I reflect with sorrow and astonishment
on the little competitions, factions, and debates of
mankind. When I read the several dates of the tombs
—of some that died yesterday, and some six hundred
years ago—I consider that great day when we shall
all of us be contemporaries, and make our appearance
together.

On Cowley and Montaigne

Præsens, absens ut sies.—Ter., *Eun.*, Act I. Sc. ii.

It is a hard and nice subject for a man to speak of
himself, says Cowley; it grates his own heart to say
anything of disparagement, and the reader's ears to
hear anything of praise from him. Let the tenor of
his discourse be what it will upon this subject, it generally proceeds from vanity. An ostentatious man will
rather relate a blunder or an absurdity he has com-

mitted, than be debarred from talking of his own dear person.

Some very great writers have been guilty of this fault. It is observed of Tully in particular, that his works run very much in the first person, and that he takes all occasions of doing himself justice. " Does he think," says Brutus, " that his consulship deserves more applause than my putting Cæsar to death, because I am not perpetually talking of the Ides of March, as he is of the Nones of December ? " I need not acquaint my learned reader, that in the Ides of March Brutus destroyed Cæsar, and that Cicero quashed the conspiracy of Cataline in the calends of December. How shocking soever this great man's talking of himself might have been to his contemporaries, I must confess I am never better pleased than when he is on this subject. Such openings of the heart give a man a thorough insight into his personal character, and illustrate several passages in the history of his life : besides that there is some little pleasure in discovering the infirmity of a great man, and seeing how the opinion he has of himself agrees with what the world entertains of him.

The gentlemen of Port Royal, who were more eminent for their learning and their humility than any other in France, banished the way of speaking in the first person out of all their works, as arising from vainglory and self-conceit. To show their particular aversion to it, they branded this form of writing with the name of an *egotism ;* a figure not to be found among the ancient rhetoricians.

The most violent egotism which I have met with in the course of my reading, is that of Cardinal Wolsey, *Ego et rex meus* (I and my king) ; as perhaps the most eminent egotist that ever appeared in the world was Montaigne, the author of the celebrated essays. This lively old Gascon has woven all his bodily infirmities into his works, and after having spoken of the faults or virtues of any other man, immediately publishes to the world how it stands with himself in that particular. Had he kept his own counsel he might have passed for a much better man, though perhaps he would not have been so diverting an author. The title of an essay promises perhaps a discourse upon Virgil or Julius Cæsar ; but when you look into it, you are sure to meet with more upon Monsieur Montaigne, than of either of them. The younger Scaliger, who seems to have been no great friend to this author, after having acquainted the world that his father sold herrings, adds these words : " La grande fadaise de Montaigne, Qui a escrit, qu'il aimoit mieux le vin blanc——Que diable a-t-on à faire de scavoir ce qu'il aime ? " " For my part," says Montaigne, " I am a great lover of your white wines." " What the devil signifies it to the public," says Scaliger, " whether he is a lover of white wines or of red wines ? "

I cannot here forbear mentioning a tribe of egotists for whom I have always had a mortal aversion ; I mean the authors of memoirs, who are never mentioned in any works but their own, and who raise all their productions out of this single figure of speech.

Most of our modern prefaces savour very strongly of the egotism. Every insignificant author fancies it of importance to the world, to know that he writ his book in the country, that he did it to pass away some of his idle hours, that it was published at the importunity of friends, or that his natural temper, studies, or conversations directed him to the choice of his subject.

" Id populus curat scilicet."

Such informations cannot but be highly improving to the reader.

In works of humour, especially when a man writes

under a fictitious personage, the talking of one's self may give some diversion to the public ; but I would advise every other writer never to speak of himself, unless there be something very considerable in his character : though I am sensible this rule will be of little use in the world, because there is no man who fancies his thoughts worth publishing that does not look upon himself as a considerable person.

I shall close this paper with a remark upon such as are egotists in conversation : these are generally the vain or shallow part of mankind, people being naturally full of themselves when they have nothing else in them. There is one kind of egotists which is very common in the world, though I do not remember that any writer has taken notice of them ; I mean those empty conceited fellows, who repeat as sayings of their own, or some of their particular friends, several jests which were made before they were born, and which every one who has conversed in the world has heard a hundred times over. A forward young fellow of my acquaintance was very guilty of this absurdity. He would be always laying a new scene for some old piece of wit, and telling us, that as he and Jack Such-a-one were together, one or t'other of them had such a conceit on such an occasion ; upon which he would laugh very heartily, and wonder the company did not join with him. When his mirth was over, I have often reprehended him out of Terence, "Tuumne, obsecro te, hoc dictum erat ? vetus credidi." But finding him still incorrigible, and having a kindness for the young coxcomb, who was otherwise a good-natured fellow, I recommended to his perusal the Oxford and Cambridge *Jests*, with several little pieces of pleasantry of the same nature. Upon the reading of them, he was under no small confusion to find that all his jokes had passed through several editions, and that what he thought was a new conceit, and had appropriated to his own use, had appeared in print before he or his ingenious friends were ever heard of. This had so good an effect upon him, that he is content at present to pass for a man of plain sense in his ordinary conversation, and is never facetious but when he knows his company.

OLIVER GOLDSMITH

On National Prejudices

As I am one of that sauntering tribe of mortals who spend the greatest part of their time in taverns, coffee-houses, and other places of public resort, I have thereby an opportunity of observing an infinite variety of characters, which to a person of a contemplative turn is a much higher entertainment than a view of all the curiosities of art or nature. In one of these my late rambles I accidentally fell into a company of half a dozen gentlemen, who were engaged in a warm dispute about some political affair, the decision of which, as they were equally divided in their sentiments, they thought proper to refer to me, which naturally drew me in for a share of the conversation.

Amongst a multiplicity of other topics, we took occasion to talk of the different characters of the several nations of Europe ; when one of the gentlemen, cocking his hat, and assuming such an air of importance as if he had possessed all the merit of the English nation in his own person, declared, that the Dutch were a parcel of avaricious wretches ; the French a set of flattering sycophants ; that the Germans were drunken sots, and beastly gluttons ; and the Spaniards proud, haughty, and surly tyrants ; but that in bravery, generosity, clemency, and in every other virtue, the English excelled all the world.

This very learned and judicious remark was received with a general smile of approbation by all the company—all, I mean, but your humble servant, who, endeavouring to keep my gravity as well as I could, and reclining my head upon my arm, continued for some time in a posture of affected thoughtfulness, as if I had been musing on something else, and did not seem to attend to the subject of conversation ; hoping by this means to avoid the disagreeable necessity of explaining myself, and thereby depriving the gentleman of his imaginary happiness.

But my pseudo-patriot had no mind to let me escape so easily. Not satisfied that his opinion should pass without contradiction, he was determined to have it ratified by the suffrage of every one in the company ; for which purpose, addressing himself to me with an air of inexpressible confidence, he asked me if I was not of the same way of thinking. As I am never forward in giving my opinion, especially when I have reason to believe that it will not be agreeable ; so, when I am obliged to give it, I always hold it for a maxim to speak my real sentiments. I therefore told him that, for my own part, I should not have ventured to talk in such a peremptory strain unless I had made the tour of Europe, and examined the manners of these several nations with great care and accuracy : that perhaps a more impartial judge would not scruple to affirm, that the Dutch were more frugal and industrious, the French more temperate and polite, the Germans more hardy and patient of labour and fatigue, and the Spaniards more staid and sedate, than the English ; who, though undoubtedly brave and generous, were at the same time rash, headstrong, and impetuous ; too apt to be elated with prosperity, and to despond in adversity.

I could easily perceive, that all the company began to regard me with a jealous eye before I had finished my answer, which I had no sooner done, than the patriotic gentleman observed, with a contemptuous sneer, that he was greatly surprised how some people could have the conscience to live in a country which they did not love, and to enjoy the protection of a government to which in their hearts they were inveterate enemies. Finding that by this modest declaration of my sentiments I had forfeited the good opinion of my companions, and given them occasion to call my political principles in question, and well knowing that it was in vain to argue with men who were so very full of themselves, I threw down my reckoning and retired to my own lodgings, reflecting on the absurd and ridiculous nature of national prejudice and prepossession.

Among all the famous sayings of antiquity, there is none that does greater honour to the author, or affords greater pleasure to the reader, (at least if he be a person of a generous and benevolent heart,) than that of the philosopher who, being asked what countryman he was, replied, that he was " a citizen of the world." How few are there to be found in modern times who can say the same, or whose conduct is consistent with such a profession ! We are now become so much Englishmen, Frenchmen, Dutchmen, Spaniards, or Germans, that we are no longer citizens of the world ; so much the natives of one particular spot, or members of one petty society, that we no longer consider ourselves as the general inhabitants of the globe, or members of that grand society which comprehends the whole human kind.

Did these prejudices prevail only among the meanest and lowest of the people, perhaps they might be excused, as they have few, if any, opportunities of correcting them by reading, travelling, or conversing with foreigners : but the misfortune is, that they infect the minds, and influence the conduct, even of our gentlemen ; of those, I mean, who have every title to this appellation but an exemption from prejudice, which, however, in my opinion, ought to be regarded as the characteristical mark of a gentleman ;

for let a man's birth be ever so high, his station ever so exalted, or his fortune ever so large, yet if he is not free from national and other prejudices, I should make bold to tell him, that he had a low and vulgar mind, and had no just claim to the character of a gentleman. And, in fact, you will always find that those are most apt to boast of national merit, who have little or no merit of their own to depend on ; than which, to be sure, nothing is more natural : the slender vine twists around the sturdy oak, for no other reason in the world but because it has not strength sufficient to support itself.

Should it be alleged in defence of national prejudice, that it is the natural and necessary growth of love to our country, and that therefore the former cannot be destroyed without hurting the latter, I answer that this is a gross fallacy and delusion. That it is the growth of love to our country, I will allow ; but that it is the natural and necessary growth of it, I absolutely deny. Superstition and enthusiasm, too, are the growth of religion ; but who ever took it in his head to affirm, that they are the necessary growth of this noble principle ? They are, if you will, the bastard sprouts of this heavenly plant, but not its natural and genuine branches, and may safely enough be lopped off, without doing any harm to the parent stock : nay, perhaps, till once they are lopped off, this goodly tree can never flourish in perfect health and vigour.

Is it not very possible that I may love my own country, without hating the natives of other countries? that I may exert the most heroic bravery, the most undaunted resolution, in defending its laws and liberty, without despising all the rest of the world as cowards and poltroons ? Most certainly it is ; and if it were not—But why need I suppose what is absolutely impossible ?—But if it were not, I must own I should prefer the title of the ancient philosopher, viz., a citizen of the world, to that of an Englishman, a Frenchman, an European, or to any other appellation whatever.

History of a Poet's Garden

OF all men who form gay illusions of distant happiness, perhaps a poet is the most sanguine. Such is the ardour of his hopes, that they often are equal to actual enjoyment ; and he feels more in expectance than actual fruition. I have often regarded a character of this kind with some degree of envy. A man possessed of such warm imagination commands all nature, and arrogates possessions of which the owner has a blunter relish. While life continues, the alluring prospect lies before him ; he travels in the pursuit with confidence, and resigns it only with his last breath.

It is this happy confidence which gives life its true relish, and keeps up our spirits amidst every distress and disappointment. How much less would be done, if a man knew how little he can do ! How wretched a creature would he be if he saw the end as well as the beginning of his projects ! He would have nothing left but to sit down in torpid despair, and exchange employment for actual calamity.

I was led into this train of thinking upon lately visiting the beautiful gardens of the late Mr. Shenstone, who was himself a poet, and possessed of that warm imagination which made him ever foremost in the pursuit of flying happiness. Could he but have foreseen the end of all his schemes, for whom he was improving, and what changes his designs were to undergo, he would have scarcely amused his innocent life with what, for several years, employed him in a most harmless manner, and abridged his scanty fortune. As the progress of this improvement is a true picture of sublunary vicissitude, I could not help calling up my imagination, which, while I walked pensively along, suggested the following Reverie.

As I was turning my back upon a beautiful piece of water, enlivened with cascades and rock-work, and entering a dark walk, by which ran a prattling brook, the Genius of the place appeared before me, but more resembling the God of Time, than him more peculiarly appointed to the care of gardens. Instead of shears he bore a scythe ; and he appeared rather with the implements of husbandry than those of a modern gardener. Having remembered this place in its pristine beauty, I could not help condoling with him on its present ruinous situation. I spoke to him of the many alterations which had been made, and all for the worse; of the many shades which had been taken away, of the bowers that were destroyed by neglect, and the hedge-rows that were spoiled by clipping. The Genius, with a sigh, received my condolement, and assured me that he was equally a martyr to ignorance and taste, to refinement and rusticity. Seeing me desirous of knowing farther, he went on :

" You see, in the place before you, the paternal inheritance of a poet ; and, to a man content with little, fully sufficient for his subsistence : but a strong imagination, and a long acquaintance with the rich, are dangerous foes to contentment. Our poet, instead of sitting down to enjoy life, resolved to prepare for its future enjoyment, and set about converting a place of profit into a scene of pleasure. This he at first supposed could be accomplished at a small expense ; and he was willing for a while to stint his income, to have an opportunity of displaying his taste. The improvement in this manner went forward ; one beauty attained led him to wish for some other ; but he still hoped that every emendation would be the last. It was now therefore found, that the Improvement exceeded the subsidy—that the place was grown too large and too fine for the inhabitant. But that pride which was once exhibited could not retire ; the garden was made for the owner, and though it was become unfit for him, he could not willingly resign it to another. Thus the first idea, of its beauties contributing to the happiness of his life, was found unfaithful ; so that, instead of looking within for satisfaction, he began to think of having recourse to the praises of those who came to visit his Improvement.

" In consequence of this hope, which now took possession of his mind, the gardens were opened to the visits of every stranger ; and the country flocked round to walk, to criticize, to admire, and to do mischief. He soon found that the admirers of his taste left by no means such strong marks of their applause, as the envious did of their malignity. All the windows of his temples and the walls of his retreats were impressed with the characters of profaneness, ignorance, and obscenity ; his hedges were broken, his statues and urns defaced, and his lawns worn bare. It was now, therefore, necessary to shut up the gardens once more, and to deprive the public of that happiness which had before ceased to be his own.

" In this situation the poet continued for a time, in the character of a jealous lover, fond of the beauty he keeps, but unable to supply the extravagance of every demand. The garden by this time was completely grown and finished ; the marks of art were covered up by the luxuriance of nature ; the winding walks were grown dark ; the brook assumed a natural sylvage ; and the rocks were covered with moss. Nothing now remained but to enjoy the beauties of the place, when the poor poet died, and his garden was obliged to be sold for the benefit of those who had contributed to its embellishment.

" The beauties of the place had now for some time been celebrated as well in prose as in verse ; and all men of taste wished for so envied a spot, where every turn was marked with the poet's pencil, and every walk awakened genius and meditation. The first purchaser was one Mr. Truepenny, a button maker, who was possessed of three thousand pounds, and was willing also to be possessed of taste and genius.

" As the poet's ideas were for the natural wildness of the landscape, the button maker's were for the more regular productions of art. He conceived, perhaps, that as it is a beauty in a button to be of a regular pattern, so the same regularity ought to obtain in a landscape. Be this as it will, he employed the shears to some purpose ; he clipped up the hedges, cut down the gloomy walks, made vistas upon the stables and hog-sties, and showed his friends that a man of taste should always be doing.

" The next candidate for taste and genius was a captain of a ship, who bought the garden because the former possessor could find nothing more to mend : but unfortunately he had taste too. His great passion lay in building, in making Chinese temples and cage-work summer-houses. As the place before had an appearance of retirement and inspired meditation, he gave it a more peopled air ; every turning presented a cottage, or ice-house, or a temple ; the Improvement was converted into a little city, and it only wanted inhabitants to give it the air of a village in the East Indies.

" In this manner, in less than ten years, the Improvement has gone through the hands of as many proprietors, who were all willing to have taste, and to show their taste too. As the place had received its best finishing from the hand of the first possessor, so every innovator only lent a hand to do mischief. Those parts which were obscure, have been enlightened ; those walks which led naturally, have been twisted into serpentine windings. The colour of the flowers of the field is not more various than the variety of tastes that have been employed here, and

all in direct contradiction to the original aim of the
first improver. Could the original possessor but
revive, with what a sorrowful heart would he look
upon his favourite spot again ! He would scarcely
recollect a Dryad or a Wood-nymph of his former
acquaintance, and might perhaps find himself as much
a stranger in his own plantation as in the deserts of
Siberia.''

CHARLES LAMB

Christ's Hospital

FIVE AND THIRTY YEARS AGO

In Mr. Lamb's " Works," published a year or two since, I find a magnificent eulogy on my old school, such as it was, or now appears to him to have been, between the years 1782 and 1789. It happens, very oddly, that my own standing at Christ's was nearly corresponding with his ; and, with all gratitude to him for his enthusiasm for the cloisters, I think he has contrived to bring together whatever can be said in praise of them, dropping all the other side of the argument most ingeniously.

I remember L. at school ; and can well recollect that he had some peculiar advantages, which I and others of his schoolfellows had not. His friends lived in town, and were near at hand : and he had the privilege of going to see them, almost as often as he wished, through some invidious distinction, which was denied to us. The present worthy sub-treasurer to the Inner Temple can explain how that happened. He had his tea and hot rolls in a morning, while we were battening upon our quarter of a penny loaf— our *crug*—moistened with attenuated small beer, in wooden piggins, smacking of the pitched leathern jack it was poured from. Our Monday's milk porritch, blue and tasteless, and the pease soup of Saturday, coarse and choking, were enriched for him with a

slice of " extraordinary bread and butter," from the
hot-loaf of the Temple. The Wednesday's mess of
millet, somewhat less repugnant (we had three banyan
to four meat days in the week)—was endeared to his
palate with a lump of double-refined, and a smack of
ginger (to make it go down the more glibly) or the
fragrant cinnamon. In lieu of our *half-pickled* Sun-
days, or *quite fresh* boiled beef on Thursdays (strong
as *caro equina*), with detestable marigolds floating in
the pail to poison the broth—our scanty mutton scrags
on Fridays—and rather more savoury, but grudging,
portions of the same flesh, rotten-roasted or rare, on
the Tuesdays (the only dish which excited our appetites, and disappointed our stomachs, in almost equal
proportion)—he had his hot plate of roast veal, or
the more tempting griskin (exotics unknown to our
palates), cooked in the paternal kitchen (a great thing),
and brought him daily by his maid or aunt ! I remember the good old relative (in whom love forbade
pride) squatting down upon some odd stone in a by-
nook of the cloisters, disclosing the viands (of higher
regale than those cates which the ravens ministered
to the Tishbite) ; and the contending passions of L.
at the unfolding. There was love for the bringer ;
shame for the thing brought, and the manner of its
bringing ; sympathy for those who were too many to
share in it ; and, at top of all, hunger (eldest, strongest of the passions !) predominant, breaking down
the stony fences of shame, and awkwardness, and a
troubling over-consciousness.

I was a poor friendless boy. My parents, and those
who should care for me, were far away. Those few
acquaintances of theirs, which they could reckon upon
as being kind to me in the great city, after a little
forced notice, which they had the grace to take of me
on my first arrival in town, soon grew tired of my
holiday visits. They seemed to them to recur too
often, though I thought them few enough ; and, one

after another, they all failed me, and I felt myself alone among six hundred playmates.

O the cruelty of separating a poor lad from his early homestead ! The yearnings which I used to have towards it in those unfledged years ! How, in my dreams, would my native town (far in the west) come back, with its church, and trees, and faces ! How I would wake weeping, and in the anguish of my heart exclaim upon sweet Calne in Wiltshire !

To this late hour of my life, I trace impressions left by the recollection of those friendless holidays. The long warm days of summer never return but they bring with them a gloom from the haunting memory of those *whole-day-leaves*, when, by some strange arrangement, we were turned out, for the live-long day, upon our own hands, whether we had friends to go to, or none. I remember those bathing-excursions to the New River, which L. recalls with such relish, better, I think, than he can—for he was a home-seeking lad, and did not much care for such water-pastimes :—How merrily we would sally forth into the fields ; and strip under the first warmth of the sun ; and wanton like young dace in the streams ; getting us appetites for noon, which those of us that were penniless (our scanty morning crust long since exhausted) had not the means of allaying—while the cattle, and the birds, and the fishes, were at feed about us, and we had nothing to satisfy our cravings—the very beauty of the day, and the exercise of the pastime, and the sense of liberty, setting a keener edge upon them !— How faint and languid, finally, we would return, towards night-fall, to our desired morsel, half-rejoicing, half-reluctant, that the hours of our uneasy liberty had expired !

It was worse in the days of winter, to go prowling about the streets objectless—shivering at cold windows of print shops, to extract a little amusement ; or haply, as a last resort, in the hopes of a little novelty, to pay a fifty-times repeated visit (where our individual faces should be as well known to the warden as those of his own charges) to the Lions in the Tower—to whose levée, by courtesy immemorial, we had a prescriptive title to admission.

L.'s governor (so we called the patron who presented us to the foundation) lived in a manner under his paternal roof. Any complaint which he had to make was sure of being attended to. This was understood at Christ's, and was an effectual screen to him against the severity of masters, or worse tyranny of the monitors. The oppressions of these young brutes are heart-sickening to call to recollection. I have been called out of my bed, and *waked for the purpose*, in the coldest winter nights—and this not once, but night after night—in my shirt, to receive the discipline of a leathern thong, with eleven other sufferers, because it pleased my callow overseer, when there has been any talking heard after we were gone to bed, to make the six last beds in the dormitory, where the youngest children of us slept, answerable for an offence they neither dared to commit, nor had the power to hinder.—The same execrable tyranny drove the younger part of us from the fires, when our feet were perishing with snow ; and, under the cruelest penalties, forbade the indulgence of a drink of water, when we lay in sleepless summer nights, fevered with the season, and the day's sports.

There was one H——, who, I learned in after days, was seen expiating some maturer offence in the hulks. (Do I flatter myself in fancying that this might be the planter of that name, who suffered—at Nevis, I think, or St. Kitts,—some few years since ? My friend Tobin was the benevolent instrument of bringing him to the gallows.) This petty Nero actually branded a boy, who had offended him, with a red-hot iron ; and nearly starved forty of us, with exacting contributions, to the one half of our bread, to pamper a young

ass, which, incredible as it may seem, with the conniv-
ance of the nurse's daughter (a young flame of his) he
had contrived to smuggle in, and keep upon the leads
of the *ward*, as they called our dormitories. This
game went on for better than a week, till the foolish
beast, not able to fare well but he must cry roast
meat—happier than Caligula's minion, could he have
kept his own counsel—but, foolisher, alas ! than any
of his species in the fables—waxing fat and kicking,
in the fulness of bread, one unlucky minute would
needs proclaim his good fortune to the world below ;
and, laying out his simple throat, blew such a ram's
horn blast, as (toppling down the walls of his own
Jericho) set concealment any longer at defiance. The
client was dismissed, with certain attentions, to
Smithfield ; but I never understood that the patron
underwent any censure on the occasion. This was in
the stewardship of L.'s admired Perry.

Under the same *facile* administration, can L. have
forgotten the cool impunity with which the nurses
used to carry away openly, in open platters, for their
own tables, one out of two of every hot joint, which
the careful matron had been seeing scrupulously
weighed out for our dinners ? These things were
daily practised in that magnificent apartment, which
L. (grown connoisseur since, we presume) praises so
highly for the grand paintings " by Verrio and others,"
with which it is " hung round and adorned." But
the sight of sleek well-fed blue-coat boys in pictures
was, at that time, I believe, little consolatory to him,
or us, the living ones, who saw the better part of our
provisions carried away before our faces by harpies ;
and ourselves reduced (with the Trojan in the hall of
Dido)

> To feed our mind with idle portraiture.

L. has recorded the repugnance of the school to *gags*,
or the fat of fresh beef boiled ; and sets it down to

some superstition. But these unctuous morsels are never grateful to young palates (children are universally fat-haters), and in strong, coarse, boiled meats, *unsalted*, are detestable. A *gag-eater* in our time was equivalent to a *goule*, and held in equal detestation. —— suffered under the imputation:

> . . . . 'Twas said
> He ate strange flesh.

He was observed, after dinner, carefully to gather up the remnants left at his table (not many, nor very choice fragments, you may credit me)—and, in an especial manner, these disreputable morsels, which he would convey away, and secretly stow in the settle that stood at his bedside. None saw when he ate them. It was rumoured that he privately devoured them in the night. He was watched, but no traces of such midnight practices were discoverable. Some reported, that, on leave-days, he had been seen to carry out of the bounds a large blue check handkerchief, full of something. This then must be the accursed thing. Conjecture next was at work to imagine how he could dispose of it. Some said he sold it to the beggars. This belief generally prevailed. He went about moping. None spake to him. No one would play with him. He was excommunicated ; put out of the pale of the school. He was too powerful a boy to be beaten, but he underwent every mode of that negative punishment, which is more grievous than many stripes. Still he persevered. At length he was observed by two of his schoolfellows, who were determined to get at the secret, and had traced him one leave-day for the purpose, to enter a large worn-out building, such as there exist specimens of in Chancery Lane, which are let out to various scales of pauperism, with open door, and a common staircase. After him they silently slunk in, and followed by stealth up four flights, and saw him tap at a poor wicket, which was opened by an aged woman, meanly clad. Suspicion was now ripened into certainty. The informers had secured their victim. They had him in their toils. Accusation was formally preferred, and retribution most signal was looked for. Mr. Hathaway, the then steward (for this happened a little after my time), with that patient sagacity which tempered all his conduct, determined to investigate the matter, before he proceeded to sentence. The result was, that the supposed mendicants, the receivers or purchasers of the mysterious scraps, turned out to be the parents of ———, an honest couple come to decay,—whom this seasonable supply had, in all probability, saved from mendicancy ; and that this young stork, at the expense of his own good name, had all this while been only feeding the old birds !—The governors on this occasion, much to their honour, voted a present relief to the family of ———, and presented him with a silver medal.

The lesson which the steward read upon RASH JUDGMENT, on the occasion of publicly delivering the medal to ———, I believe, would not be lost upon his auditory.—I had left school then, but I well remember ———. He was a tall, shambling youth, with a cast in his eye, not at all calculated to conciliate hostile prejudices. I have since seen him carrying a baker's basket. I think I heard he did not do quite so well by himself as he had done by the old folks.

I was a hypochondriac lad ; and the sight of a boy in fetters, upon the day of my first putting on the blue clothes, was not exactly fitted to assuage the natural terrors of initiation. I was of tender years, barely turned of seven ; and had only read of such things in books, or seen them but in dreams. I was told he had *run away*. This was the punishment for the first offence.—As a novice I was soon after taken to see the dungeons. These were little, square, Bedlam cells, where a boy could just lie at his length upon straw and a blanket—a mattress, I think, was afterwards substituted—with a peep of light, let in askance, from a prison-orifice at top, barely enough to read by. Here the poor boy was locked in by himself all day, without sight of any but the porter who brought him his bread and water—who *might not speak to him ;*— or of the beadle, who came twice a week to call him out to receive his periodical chastisement, which was almost welcome, because it separated him for a brief interval from solitude :—and here he was shut up by himself *of nights*, out of the reach of any sound, to suffer whatever horrors the weak nerves, and superstition incident to his time of life, might subject him to. This was the penalty for the second offence. Wouldst thou like, reader, to see what became of him in the next degree ?

The culprit who had been a third time an offender, and whose expulsion was at this time deemed irreversible, was brought forth, as at some solemn *auto da fé*, arrayed in uncouth and most appalling attire, all trace of his late " watchet-weeds " carefully effaced ; he was exposed in a jacket, resembling those which London lamplighters formerly delighted in, with a cap of the same. The effect of this divestiture was such as the ingenious devisers of it could have anticipated. With his pale and frighted features, it was as if some of those disfigurements in Dante had seized upon him. In this disguisement he was brought into the hall (*L.'s favourite state-room*), where awaited him the whole number of his schoolfellows, whose joint lessons and sports he was thenceforth to share no more ; the awful presence of the steward, to be seen for the last time ; of the executioner beadle, clad in his state robe for the occasion ; and of two faces more, of direr import, because never but in these extremities visible. These were governors ; two of whom, by choice, or charter, were always accustomed to officiate at these *Ultima Supplicia ;* not to mitigate (so at least we understood it), but to enforce the uttermost stripe. Old Bamber Gascoigne, and Peter Aubert, I remember, were colleagues on one occasion, when the beadle turning rather pale, a glass of brandy was ordered to prepare him for the mysteries. The scourging was, after the old Roman fashion, long and stately. The lictor accompanied the criminal quite round the hall. We were generally too faint with attending to the previous disgusting circumstances to make accurate report with our eyes of the degree of corporal suffering inflicted. Report, of course, gave out the back knotty and livid. After scourging, he was made over, in his *San Benito*, to his friends, if he had any (but commonly such poor runagates were friendless), or to his parish officer, who, to enhance the effect of the scene, had his station allotted to him on the outside of the hall gate.

These solemn pageantries were not played off so often as to spoil the general mirth of the community. We had plenty of exercise and recreation *after* school hours ; and, for myself, I must confess, that I was never happier than *in* them. The Upper and the Lower Grammar Schools were held in the same room ; and an imaginary line only divided their bounds. Their character was as different as that of the inhabitants on the two sides of the Pyrenees. The Rev. James Boyer was the Upper Master ; but the Rev. Matthew Feilde presided over that portion of the apartment of which I had the good fortune to be a member. We lived a life as careless as birds. We talked and did just what we pleased, and nobody molested us. We carried an accidence, or a grammar, for form ; but, for any trouble it gave us, we might take two years in getting through the verbs deponent, and another two in forgetting all that we had learned about them. There was now and then the formality of saying a lesson, but if you had not learned it, a brush across the shoulders (just enough to disturb a fly) was the sole remonstrance. Feilde never used the rod ; and in truth he wielded the cane with no great good will—holding it " like a dancer." It looked in his hands rather like an emblem than an instrument of authority ; and an emblem, too, he was ashamed of. He was a good easy man, that did not care to ruffle his own peace, nor perhaps set any great consideration upon the value of juvenile time. He came among us, now and then, but often staid away whole days from us ; and when he came, it made no difference to us—he had his private room to retire to, the short time he staid, to be out of the sound of our noise. Our mirth and uproar went on. We had classics of our own, without being beholden to " insolent Greece or haughty Rome," that passed current among us—Peter Wilkins—the Adventures of the Hon. Captain Robert Boyle—the Fortunate Bluecoat Boy—and the like. Or we cultivated a turn for mechanic and scientific operations ; making little sundials of paper ; or weaving those ingenious parentheses, called *cat-cradles ;* or making dry peas to dance upon the end of a tin pipe ; or studying the art military over that laudable game " French and English," and a hundred other such devices to pass away the time—mixing the useful with the agreeable—as would have made the souls of Rousseau and John Locke chuckle to have seen us.

Matthew Feilde belonged to that class of modest divines who affect to mix in equal proportion the *gentleman*, the *scholar*, and the *Christian ;* but, I know not how, the first ingredient is generally found to be the predominating dose in the composition. He was engaged in gay parties, or with his courtly bow at some episcopal levée, when he should have been attending upon us. He had for many years the classical charge of a hundred children, during the four or five first years of their education ; and his very highest form seldom proceeded further than two or three of the introductory fables of Phædrus. How things were suffered to go on thus, I cannot guess. Boyer, who was the proper person to have remedied these abuses, always affected, perhaps felt, a delicacy in interfering in a province not strictly his own. I have not been without my suspicions, that he was not altogether displeased at the contrast we presented to his end of the school. We were a sort of Helots to his young Spartans. He would sometimes, with ironic deference, send to borrow a rod of the Under Master, and then, with sardonic grin, observe to one of his upper boys, " how neat and fresh the twigs looked." While his pale students were battering their brains over Xenophon and Plato, with a silence as deep as that enjoined by the Samite, we were enjoying ourselves at our ease in our little Goshen. We saw a little into the secrets of his discipline, and the prospect did but the more reconcile us to our lot. His thunders rolled innocuous for us ; his storms came near, but never touched us ; contrary to Gideon's miracle, while all around were drenched, our fleece was dry. His boys turned out the better scholars ; we, I suspect, have the advantage in temper. His pupils cannot speak of him without something of terror allaying their gratitude ; the remembrance of Feilde comes back with all the soothing images of indolence, and summer slumbers, and work like play, and innocent idleness, and Elysian exemptions, and life itself a " playing holiday."

Though sufficiently removed from the jurisdiction of Boyer, we were near enough (as I have said) to understand a little of his system. We occasionally heard sounds of the *Ululantes*, and caught glances of Tartarus. B. was a rabid pedant. His English style was crampt to barbarism. His Easter anthems (for his duty obliged him to those periodical flights) were grating as scrannel pipes.—He would laugh—ay, and heartily—but then it must be at Flaccus's quibble about *Rex*—— or at the *tristris severitas in vultu*, or *inspicere in patinas*, of Terence—thin jests, which at their first broaching could hardly have had *vis* enough to move a Roman muscle.—He had two wigs, both pedantic, but of different omen. The one serene, smiling, fresh powdered, betokening a mild day. The other, an old discoloured, unkempt, angry caxon, denoting frequent and bloody execution. Woe to the school, when he made his morning appearance in his *passy*, or *passionate wig*. No comet expounded surer. —J. B. had a heavy hand. I have known him double his knotty fist at a poor trembling child (the maternal milk hardly dry upon its lips) with a " Sirrah, do you presume to set your wits at me ? "—Nothing was more common than to see him make a headlong entry into the school-room, from his inner recess, or library, and, with turbulent eye, singling out a lad, roar out, " Od's my life, sirrah " (his favourite adjuration), " I have a great mind to whip you,"—then, with as sudden a retracting impulse, fling back into his lair— and, after a cooling lapse of some minutes (during which all but the culprit had totally forgotten the context) drive headlong out again, piecing out his imperfect sense, as if it had been some Devil's Litany, with the expletory yell—" *and I* WILL *too*."—In his gentler moods, when the *rabidus furor* was assuaged, he had resort to an ingenious method, peculiar, for what I have heard, to himself, of whipping the boy, and reading the Debates, at the same time ; a paragraph and a lash between ; which in those times, when parliamentary oratory was most at a height and flourishing in these realms, was not calculated to impress the patient with a veneration for the diffuser graces of rhetoric.

Once, and but once, the uplifted rod was known to fall ineffectual from his hand—when droll squinting W—— having been caught putting the inside of the master's desk to a use for which the architect had

clearly not designed it, to justify himself, with great
simplicity averred, that *he did not know that the thing
had been forewarned*. This exquisite irrecognition of
any law antecedent to the *oral* or *declaratory*, struck
so irresistibly upon the fancy of all who heard it (the
pedagogue himself not excepted) that remission was
unavoidable.

L. has given credit to B.'s great merits as an in-
structor. Coleridge, in his literary life, has pronounced
a more intelligible and ample encomium on them.
The author of the *Country Spectator* doubts not to
compare him with the ablest teachers of antiquity.
Perhaps we cannot dismiss him better than with the
pious ejaculation of C.—when he heard that his old
master was on his death-bed : " Poor J. B. !—may
all his faults be forgiven ; and may he be wafted to
bliss by little cherub boys, all head and wings, with
no *bottoms* to reproach his sublunary infirmities."

Under him were many good and sound scholars
bred.—First Grecian of my time was Lancelot Pepys
Stevens, kindest of boys and men, since Co-grammar-
master (and inseparable companion) with Dr. T——e.
What an edifying spectacle did this brace of friends
present to those who remembered the anti-socialities
of their predecessors !—You never met the one by
chance in the street without a wonder, which was
quickly dissipated by the almost immediate sub-
appearance of the other. Generally arm-in-arm, these
kindly coadjutors lightened for each other the toil-
some duties of their profession, and when, in advanced
age, one found it convenient to retire, the other was
not long in discovering that it suited him to lay down
the fasces also. Oh, it is pleasant, as it is rare, to find
the same arm linked in yours at forty, which at thirteen helped it to turn over the *Cicero De Amicitiâ*, or
some tale of Antique Friendship, which the young
heart even then was burning to anticipate !—Co-
Grecian with S. was Th——, who has since executed

with ability various diplomatic functions at the Northern courts. Th—— was a tall, dark, saturnine youth, sparing of speech, with raven locks.—Thomas Fanshaw Middleton followed him (now Bishop of Calcutta), a scholar and a gentleman in his teens. He has the reputation of an excellent critic ; and is author (besides the *Country Spectator*) of a Treatise on the Greek Article, against Sharpe.—M. is said to bear his mitre high in India, where the *regni novitas* (I dare say) sufficiently justifies the bearing. A humility quite as primitive as that of Jewel or Hooker might not be exactly fitted to impress the minds of those Anglo-Asiatic diocesans with a reverence for home institutions, and the church which those fathers watered. The manners of M. at school, though firm, were mild and unassuming.—Next to M. (if not senior to him) was Richards, author of the *Aboriginal Britons*, the most spirited of the Oxford Prize Poems ; a pale, studious Grecian.—Then followed poor S——, ill-fated M——! of these the Muse is silent.

> Finding some of Edward's race
> Unhappy, pass their annals by.

Come back into memory, like as thou wert in the dayspring of thy fancies, with hope like a fiery column before thee—the dark pillar not yet turned—Samuel Taylor Coleridge—Logician, Metaphysician, Bard !—How have I seen the casual passer through the Cloisters stand still, intranced with admiration (while he weighed the disproportion between the *speech* and the *garb* of the young Mirandula), to hear thee unfold, in thy deep and sweet intonations, the mysteries of Jamblichus, or Plotinus (for even in those years thou waxedest not pale at such philosophic draughts), or reciting Homer in his Greek, or Pindar——while the walls of the old Grey Friars re-echoed to the accents of the *inspired charity-boy !*—

Many were the " wit-combats " (to dally awhile with the words of old Fuller), between him and C. V. Le G——, "which two I behold like a Spanish great galleon, and an English man of war : Master Coleridge, like the former, was built far higher in learning, solid, but slow in his performances. C. V. L., with the English man of war, lesser in bulk, but lighter in sailing, could turn with all times, tack about, and take advantage of all winds, by the quickness of his wit and invention."

Nor shalt thou, their compeer, be quickly forgotten, Allen, with the cordial smile, and still more cordial laugh, with which thou wert wont to make the old Cloisters shake, in thy cognition of some poignant jest of theirs ; or the anticipation of some more material, and, peradventure practical one, of thine own. Extinct are those smiles, with that beautiful countenance, with which (for thou wert the *Nireus formosus* of the school), in the days of thy maturer waggery, thou didst disarm the wrath of infuriated town-damsel, who, incensed by provoking pinch, turning tigress-like round, suddenly converted by thy angel-look, exchanged the half-formed terrible " *bl*——," for a gentler greeting—" *bless thy handsome face !* "

Next follow two, who ought to be now alive, and the friends of Elia—the junior Le G—— and F—— ; who impelled, the former by a roving temper, the latter by too quick a sense of neglect—ill capable of enduring the slights poor Sizars are sometimes subject to in our seats of learning—exchanged their Alma Mater for the camp ; perishing, one by climate, and one on the plains of Salamanca :—Le G——, sanguine, volatile, sweet-natured ; F——, dogged, faithful, anticipative of insult, warm-hearted, with something of the old Roman height about him.

Fine, frank-hearted Fr——, the present master of Hertford, with Marmaduke T—— mildest of Mission-

aries—and both my good friends still—close the
catalogue of Grecians in my time.

Imperfect Sympathies

> I am of a constitution so general, that it consorts and
> sympathiseth with all things ; I have no antipathy, or
> rather idiosyncrasy in anything. Those natural repug-
> nances do not touch me, nor do I behold with prejudice
> the French, Italian, Spaniard, or Dutch.—*Religio Medici.*

THAT the author of the *Religio Medici* mounted upon
the airy stilts of abstraction, conversant about no-
tional and conjectural essences ; in whose categories
of Being the possible took the upper hand of the
actual ; should have overlooked the impertinent in-
dividualities of such poor concretions as mankind, is
not much to be admired. It is rather to be wondered
at, that in the genus of animals he should have con-
descended to distinguish that species at all. For myself—earth-bound and fettered to the scene of my
activities,—

> Standing on earth, not rapt above the sky,

I confess that I do feel the differences of mankind,
national or individual, to an unhealthy excess. I can
look with no indifferent eye upon things or persons.
Whatever is, is to me a matter of taste or distaste ;
or when once it becomes indifferent it begins to be
disrelishing. I am, in plainer words, a bundle of prejudices—made up of likings and dislikings—the
veriest thrall to sympathies, apathies, antipathies.
In a certain sense, I hope it may be said of me that
I am a lover of my species. I can feel for all indifferently, but I cannot feel towards all equally. The
more purely-English word that expresses sympathy,
will better explain my meaning. I can be a friend to

a worthy man, who upon another account cannot be my mate or *fellow*. I cannot *like* all people alike.

I have been trying all my life to like Scotchmen, and am obliged to desist from the experiment in despair. They cannot like me—and in truth, I never knew one of that nation who attempted to do it. There is something more plain and ingenuous in their mode of proceeding. We know one another at first sight. There is an order of imperfect intellects (under which mine must be content to rank) which in its constitution is essentially anti-Caledonian. The owners of the sort of faculties I allude to, have minds rather suggestive than comprehensive. They have no pretences to much clearness or precision in their ideas, or in their manner of expressing them. Their intellectual wardrobe (to confess fairly) has few whole pieces in it. They are content with fragments and scattered pieces of Truth. She presents no full front to them—a feature or side-face at the most. Hints and glimpses, germs and crude essays at a system, is the utmost they pretend to. They beat up a little game peradventure—and leave it to knottier heads, more robust constitutions, to run it down. The light that lights them is not steady and polar, but mutable and shifting : waxing and again waning. Their conversation is accordingly. They will throw out a random word in or out of season, and be content to let it pass for what it is worth. They cannot speak always as if they were upon their oath—but must be understood, speaking or writing, with some abatement. They seldom wait to mature a proposition, but e'en bring it to market in the green ear. They delight to impart their defective discoveries as they arise, without waiting for their development. They are no systematizers, and would but err more by attempting it. Their minds, as I said before, are suggestive merely. The brain of a true Caledonian (if I am not mistaken) is constituted upon quite a different plan.

His Minerva is born in panoply. You are never admitted to see his ideas in their growth—if, indeed, they do grow, and are not rather put together upon principles of clock-work. You never catch his mind in an undress. He never hints or suggests anything, but unlades his stock of ideas in perfect order and completeness. He brings his total wealth into company, and gravely unpacks it. His riches are always about him. He never stoops to catch a glittering something in your presence to share it with you, before he quite knows whether it be true touch or not. You cannot cry *halves* to anything that he finds. He does not find, but bring. You never witness his first apprehension of a thing. His understanding is always at its meridian—you never see the first dawn, the early streaks.—He has no falterings of self-suspicion. Surmises, guesses, misgivings, half-intuitions, semi-consciousnesses, partial illuminations, dim instincts, embryo conceptions, have no place in his brain or vocabulary. The twilight of dubiety never falls upon him. Is he orthodox—he has no doubts. Is he an infidel—he has none either. Between the affirmative and the negative there is no border-land with him. You cannot hover with him upon the confines of truth, or wander in the maze of a probable argument. He always keeps the path. You cannot make excursions with him—for he sets you right. His taste never fluctuates. His morality never abates. He cannot compromise, or understand middle actions. There can be but a right and a wrong. His conversation is as a book. His affirmations have the sanctity of an oath. You must speak upon the square with him. He stops a metaphor like a suspected person in an enemy's country. " A healthy book ! "—said one of his countrymen to me, who had ventured to give that appellation to John Buncle,—" Did I catch rightly what you said ? I have heard of a man in health, and of a healthy state of body, but I do not see how that

epithet can be properly applied to a book." Above
all, you must beware of indirect expressions before a
Caledonian. Clap an extinguisher upon your irony,
if you are unhappily blest with a vein of it. Remember you are upon your oath. I have a print of a
graceful figure after Leonardo da Vinci, which I was
showing off to Mr. **** After he had examined it
minutely, I ventured to ask him how he liked MY
BEAUTY (a foolish name it goes by among my friends)
—when he very gravely assured me, that " he had considerable respect for my character and talents " (so he
was pleased to say), " but had not given himself much
thought about the degree of my personal pretensions."
The misconception staggered me, but did not seem
much to disconcert him.—Persons of this nation are
particularly fond of affirming a truth—which nobody
doubts. They do not so properly affirm, as annunci-
ate it. They do indeed appear to have such a love of
truth (as if, like virtue, it were valuable for itself) that
all truth becomes equally valuable, whether the proposition that contains it be new or old, disputed, or
such as is impossible to become a subject of dispu-
tation. I was present not long since at a party of
North Britons, where a son of Burns was expected ;
and happened to drop a silly expression (in my South
British way), that I wished it were the father instead
of the son—when four of them started up at once to
inform me, that " that was impossible, because he was
dead." An impracticable wish, it seems, was more
than they could conceive. Swift has hit off this part
of their character, namely their love of truth, in his
biting way, but with an illiberality that necessarily
confines the passage to the margin. The tediousness
of these people is certainly provoking. I wonder
if they ever tire one another !—In my early life I had
a passionate fondness for the poetry of Burns. I have
sometimes foolishly hoped to ingratiate myself with
his countrymen by expressing it. But I have always

found that a true Scot resents your admiration of his
compatriot even more than he would your contempt
of him. The latter he imputes to your " imperfect
acquaintance with many of the words which he uses;"
and the same objection makes it a presumption in you
to suppose that you can admire him.—Thomson
they seem to have forgotten. Smollett they have
neither forgotten nor forgiven, for his delineation
of Rory and his companion, upon their first intro-
duction to our metropolis.—Speak of Smollett as
a great genius, and they will retort upon you
Hume's History compared with *his* Continuation of
it. What if the historian had continued *Humphry
Clinker ?*

I have, in the abstract, no disrespect for the Jews.
They are a piece of stubborn antiquity, compared with
which Stonehenge is in its nonage. They date beyond
the pyramids. But I should not care to be in habits
of familiar intercourse with any of that nation. I
confess that I have not the nerves to enter their syna-
gogues. Old prejudices cling about me. I cannot
shake off the story of Hugh of Lincoln. Centuries
of injury, contempt, and hate, on the one side,—of
cloaked revenge, dissimulation, and hate, on the
other, between our and their fathers, must and ought
to affect the blood of the children. I cannot believe
it can run clear and kindly yet ; or that a few words,
such as candour, liberality, the light of the nineteenth
century, can close up the breaches of so deadly a dis-
union. A Hebrew is nowhere congenial to me. He
is least distasteful on 'Change—for the mercantile
spirit levels all distinctions, as all are beauties in the
dark. I boldly confess that I do not relish the approxi-
mation of Jew and Christian, which has become so
fashionable. The reciprocal endearments have, to me,
something hypocritical and unnatural in them. I do
not like to see the Church and Synagogue kissing and
congeeing in awkward postures of an affected civility.

If *they* are converted, why do they not come over to us altogether? Why keep up a form of separation, when the life of it is fled? If they can sit with us at table, why do they keck at our cookery? I do not understand these half convertites. Jews christianizing—Christians judaizing—puzzle me. I like fish or flesh. A moderate Jew is a more confounding piece of anomaly than a wet Quaker. The spirit of the synagogue is essentially *separative*. B—— would have been more in keeping if he had abided by the faith of his forefathers. There is a fine scorn in his face, which nature meant to be of——Christians.—— The Hebrew spirit is strong in him, in spite of his proselytism. He cannot conquer the Shibboleth. How it breaks out, when he sings, "The Children of Israel passed through the Red Sea!" The auditors, for the moment, are as Egyptians to him, and he rides over our necks in triumph. There is no mistaking him. B—— has a strong expression of sense in his countenance, and it is confirmed by his singing. The foundation of his vocal excellence is sense. He sings with understanding, as Kemble delivered dialogue. He would sing the Commandments, and give an appropriate character to each prohibition. His nation, in general, have not over-sensible countenances. How should they?—but you seldom see a silly expression among them.—Gain, and the pursuit of gain, sharpen a man's visage. I never heard of an idiot being born among them.—Some admire the Jewish female-physiognomy. I admire it—but with trembling. Jael had those full dark inscrutable eyes.

In the Negro countenance you will often meet with strong traits of benignity. I have felt yearnings of tenderness towards some of these faces—or rather masks—that have looked out kindly upon one in casual encounters in the streets and highways. I love what Fuller beautifully calls—these "images of God cut in ebony." But I should not like to associate

with them, to share my meals and my good nights
with them—because they are black.

I love Quaker ways, and Quaker worship. I vener-
ate the Quaker principles. It does me good for the
rest of the day when I meet any of their people in my
path. When I am ruffled or disturbed by any occur-
rence, the sight, or quiet voice of a Quaker, acts upon
me as a ventilator, lightening the air, and taking off
a load from the bosom. But I cannot like the
Quakers (as Desdemona would say) " to live with
them." I am all over sophisticated—with humours,
fancies, craving hourly sympathy. I must have
books, pictures, theatres, chit-chat, scandal, jokes,
ambiguities, and a thousand whim-whams, which
their simpler taste can do without. I should starve
at their primitive banquet. My appetites are too
high for the salads which (according to Evelyn) Eve
dressed for the angel ; my gusto too excited

> To sit a guest with Daniel at his pulse.

The indirect answers which Quakers are often found
to return to a question put to them may be explained,
I think, without the vulgar assumption, that they
are more given to evasion and equivocating than
other people. They naturally look to their words
more carefully, and are more cautious of committing
themselves. They have a peculiar character to keep
up on this head. They stand in a manner upon their
veracity. A Quaker is by law exempted from taking
an oath. The custom of resorting to an oath in
extreme cases, sanctified as it is by all religious
antiquity, is apt (it must be confessed) to introduce
into the laxer sort of minds the notion of two kinds
of truth—the one applicable to the solemn affairs of
justice, and the other to the common proceedings of
daily intercourse. As truth bound upon the conscience by an oath can be but truth, so in the common

affirmations of the shop and the market-place a latitude is expected and conceded upon questions wanting this solemn covenant. Something less than truth satisfies. It is common to hear a person say, " You do not expect me to speak as if I were upon my oath." Hence a great deal of incorrectness and inadvertency, short of falsehood, creeps into ordinary conversation ; and a kind of secondary or laic-truth is tolerated, where clergy-truth—oath-truth, by the nature of the circumstances, is not required. A Quaker knows none of this distinction. His simple affirmation being received upon the most sacred occasions, without any further test, stamps a value upon the words which he is to use upon the most in- different topics of life. He looks to them, naturally, with more severity. You can have of him no more than his word. He knows, if he is caught tripping in a casual expression, he forfeits, for himself at least, his claim to the invidious exemption. He knows that his syllables are weighed—and how far a conscious- ness of this particular watchfulness, exerted against a person, has a tendency to produce indirect answers, and a diverting of the question by honest means, might be illustrated, and the practice justified by a more sacred example than is proper to be adduced upon this occasion. The admirable presence of mind, which is notorious in Quakers upon all contingencies, might be traced to this imposed self-watchfulness— if it did not seem rather an humble and secular scion of that old stock of religious constancy, which never bent or faltered, in the Primitive Friends, or gave way to the winds of persecution, to the violence of judge or accuser, under trials and racking examina- tions. " You will never be the wiser, if I sit here answering your questions till midnight," said one of those upright Justicers to Penn, who had been putting law-cases with a puzzling subtlety. " Thereafter as the answers may be," retorted the Quaker. The

astonishing composure of this people is sometimes
ludicrously displayed in lighter instances.—I was
travelling in a stage-coach with three male Quakers,
buttoned up in the straitest nonconformity of their
sect. We stopped to bait at Andover, where a meal,
partly tea apparatus, partly supper, was set before
us. My friends confined themselves to the tea-table.
I in my way took supper. When the landlady brought
in the bill, the eldest of my companions discovered
that she had charged for both meals. This was
resisted. Mine hostess was very clamorous and positive. Some mild arguments were used on the part
of the Quakers, for which the heated mind of the
good lady seemed by no means a fit recipient. The
guard came with his usual peremptory notice. The
Quakers pulled out their money and formally tendered it—so much for tea—I, in humble imitation,
tendering mine—for the supper which I had taken.
She would not relax in her demand. So they all three
quietly put up their silver, as did myself, and marched
out of the room, the eldest and gravest going first,
with myself closing up the rear, who thought I could
not do better than follow the example of such grave
and warrantable personages. We got in. The steps
went up. The coach drove off. The murmurs of
mine hostess, not very indistinctly or ambiguously
pronounced, became after a time inaudible—and now
my conscience, which the whimsical scene had for a
while suspended, beginning to give some twitches, I
waited, in the hope that some justification would be
offered by these serious persons for the seeming in-
justice of their conduct. To my great surprise not a
syllable was dropped on the subject. They sat as
mute as at a meeting. At length the eldest of them
broke silence, by inquiring of his next neighbour,
" Hast thee heard how indigos go at the India
House ? " and the question operated as soporific on
my moral feeling as far as Exeter.

Preface to the Last Essays

By a Friend of the late Elia

THIS poor gentleman, who for some months past had been in a declining way, hath at length paid his final tribute to nature.

To say truth, it is time he were gone. The humour of the thing, if ever there was much in it, was pretty well exhausted; and a two years' and a half existence has been a tolerable duration for a phantom.

I am now at liberty to confess, that much which I have heard objected to my late friend's writings was well-founded. Crude they are, I grant you—a sort of unlicked, incondite things—villainously pranked in an affected array of antique modes and phrases. They had not been *his*, if they had been other than such; and better it is, that a writer should be natural in a self-pleasing quaintness, than to affect a naturalness (so called) that should be strange to him. Egotistical they have been pronounced by some who did not know, that what he tells us, as of himself, was often true only (historically) of another; as in a former Essay (to save many instances)—where under the *first person* (his favourite figure) he shadows forth the forlorn estate of a country-boy placed at a London school, far from his friends and connections—in direct opposition to his own early history. If it be egotism to imply and twine with his own identity the griefs and affections of another—making himself many, or reducing many unto himself—then is the skilful novelist, who all along brings in his hero or heroine, speaking of themselves, the greatest egotist of all; who yet has never, therefore, been accused of that narrowness. And how shall the intenser dramatist escape being faulty, who, doubtless, under cover of passion uttered by another, oftentimes gives blameless vent to his most inward feelings, and expresses his own story modestly ?

My late friend was in many respects a singular character. Those who did not like him, hated him ; and some, who once liked him, afterwards became his bitterest haters. The truth is, he gave himself too little concern what he uttered, and in whose presence. He observed neither time nor place, and would e'en out with what came uppermost. With the severe religionist he would pass for a free-thinker ; while the other faction set him down for a bigot, or persuaded themselves that he belied his sentiments. Few understood him ; and I am not certain that at all times he quite understood himself. He too much affected that dangerous figure—irony. He sowed doubtful speeches, and reaped plain, unequivocal hatred. He would interrupt the gravest discussion with some light jest ; and yet, perhaps, not quite irrevelant in ears that could understand it. Your long and much talkers hated him. The informal habit of his mind, joined to an inveterate impediment of speech, forbade him to be an orator ; and he seemed determined that no one else should play that part when he was present. He was *petit* and ordinary in his person and appearance. I have seen him sometimes in what is called good company, but where he has been a stranger, sit silent, and be suspected for an odd fellow ; till some unlucky occasion provoking it, he would stutter out some senseless pun (not altogether senseless, perhaps, if rightly taken), which has stamped his character for the evening. It was hit or miss with him ; but nine times out of ten, he contrived by this device to send away a whole company his enemies. His conceptions rose kindlier than his utterance, and his happiest *impromptus* had the appearance of effort. He has been accused of trying to be witty, when in truth he was but struggling to give his poor thoughts articulation. He chose his companions for some individuality of character which they manifested. Hence, not many persons of science, and few professed *literati*, were of his councils. They were, for the most part, persons of an uncertain fortune ; and, as to such people commonly nothing is more obnoxious than a gentleman of settled (though moderate) income, he passed with most of them for a great miser. To my knowledge this was a mistake. His *intimados*, to confess a truth, were in the world's eye a ragged regiment. He found them floating on the surface of society ; and the colour, or something else, in the weed pleased him. The burrs stuck to him—but they were good and loving burrs for all that. He never greatly cared for the society of what are called good people. If any of these were scandalized (and offences were sure to arise) he could not help it. When he has been remonstrated with for not making more concessions to the feelings of good people, he would retort by asking, what one point did these good people ever concede to him ? He was temperate in his meals and diversions, but always kept a little on this side of abstemiousness. Only in the use of the Indian weed he might be thought a little excessive. He took it, he would say, as a solvent of speech. Marry—as the friendly vapour ascended, how his prattle would curl up sometimes with it ! the ligaments which tongue-tied him were loosened, and the stammerer proceeded a statist !

I do not know whether I ought to bemoan or rejoice that my old friend is departed. His jests were beginning to grow obsolete, and his stories to be found out. He felt the approaches of age ; and while he pretended to cling to life, you saw how slender were the ties left to bind him. Discoursing with him latterly on this subject, he expressed himself with a pettishness, which I thought unworthy of him. In

Statist. This word once meant a politician.

our walks about his suburban retreat (as he called it) at Shacklewell, some children belonging to a school of industry had met us, and bowed and curtseyed, as he thought, in an especial manner to *him*. " They take me for a visiting governor," he muttered earnestly. He had a horror, which he carried to a foible, of looking like anything important and parochial. He thought that he approached nearer to that stamp daily. He had a general aversion from being treated like a grave or respectable character, and kept a wary eye upon the advances of age that should so entitle him. He herded always, while it was possible, with people younger than himself. He did not conform to the march of time, but was dragged along in the procession. His manners lagged behind his years. He was too much of the boy-man. The *toga virilis* never sate gracefully on his shoulders. The impressions of infancy had burnt into him, and he resented the impertinence of manhood. These were weaknesses ; but such as they were, they are a key to explicate some of his writings.

Blakesmoor in H——shire

I DO not know a pleasure more affecting than to range at will over the deserted apartments of some fine old family mansion. The traces of extinct grandeur admit of a better passion than envy : and contemplations on the great and good, whom we fancy in succession to have been its inhabitants, weave for us illusions, incompatible with the bustle of modern occupancy, and vanities of foolish present aristocracy. The same difference of feeling, I think, attends us between entering an empty and a crowded church. In the latter it is chance but some present human frailty—an act of inattention on the part of some of the auditory—or a trait of affectation, or worse, vain-glory, on that of the preacher, puts us by our best thoughts, disharmonizing the place and the occasion. But wouldst thou know the beauty of holiness ?—go alone on some week-day, borrowing the keys of good Master Sexton, traverse the cool aisles of some country church : think of the piety that has kneeled there— the congregations, old and young, that have found consolation there—the meek pastor—the docile parishioner. With no disturbing emotions, no cross conflicting comparisons, drink in the tranquillity of the place, till thou thyself become as fixed and motion- less as the marble effigies that kneel and weep around thee.

Journeying northward lately, I could not resist going some few miles out of my road to look upon the remains of an old great house with which I had been impressed in this way in infancy. I was apprised that the owner of it had lately pulled it down ; still I had a vague notion that it could not all have perished,—that so much solidity with magnificence could not have been crushed all at once into the mere dust and rubbish which I found it.

The work of ruin had proceeded with a swift hand indeed, and the demolition of a few weeks had reduced it to—an antiquity.

I was astonished at the indistinction of everything. Where had stood the great gates ? What bounded the court-yard ? Whereabout did the out-houses com- mence ? A few bricks only lay as representatives of that which was so stately and so spacious.

Death does not shrink up his human victim at this rate. The burnt ashes of a man weigh more in their proportion.

Had I seen these brick-and-mortar knaves at their process of destruction, at the plucking of every panel I should have felt the varlets at my heart. I should have cried out to them to spare a plank at least out of the cheerful store-room, in whose hot window-seat

I used to sit and read Cowley, with the grass-plot before, and the hum and flappings of that one solitary wasp that ever haunted it about me—it is in mine ears now, as oft as summer returns ; or a panel of the yellow-room.

Why, every plank and panel of that house for me had magic in it. The tapestried bedrooms—tapestry so much better than painting—not adorning merely, but peopling the wainscots—at which childhood ever and anon would steal a look, shifting its coverlid (replaced as quickly) to exercise its tender courage in a momentary eye-encounter with those stern bright visages, staring reciprocally—all Ovid on the walls, in colours vivider than his description. Actæon in mid sprout, with the unappeasable prudery of Diana ; and the still more provoking and almost culinary coolness of Dan Phœbus, eel-fashion, deliberately divesting of Marsyas.

Then, that haunted room—in which old Mrs. Battle died—whereinto I have crept, but always in the daytime, with a passion of fear ; and a sneaking curiosity, terror-tainted, to hold communication with the past.
—*How shall they build it up again ?*

It was an old deserted place, yet not so long deserted that the traces of the splendour of past inmates were everywhere apparent. Its furniture was still standing—even to the tarnished gilt leather battledores, and crumbling feathers of shuttlecocks in the nursery, which told that children had once played there. But I was a lonely child, and had the range at will of every apartment, knew every nook and corner, wondered and worshipped everywhere.

The solitude of childhood is not so much the mother of thought as it is the feeder of love, of silence, and admiration. So strange a passion for the place possessed me in those years, that, though there lay— I shame to say how few roods distant from the mansion—half hid by trees, what I judged some romantic lake, such was the spell which bound me to the house, and such my carefulness not to pass its strict and proper precincts, that the idle waters lay unexplored for me ; and not till late in life, curiosity prevailing over elder devotion, I found, to my astonishment, a pretty brawling brook had been the Lacus Incognitus of my infancy. Variegated views, extensive prospects —and those at no great distance from the house— I was told of such—what were they to me, being out of the boundaries of my Eden ? So far from a wish to roam, I would have drawn, methought, still closer the fences of my chosen prison, and have been hemmed in by a yet securer cincture of those excluding garden walls. I could have exclaimed with the garden-loving poet—

> Bind me, ye woodbines, in your twines ;
> Curl me about, ye gadding vines ;
> And oh so close your circles lace,
> That I may never leave this place ;
> But, lest your fetters prove too weak,
> Ere I your silken bondage break,
> Do you, O brambles, chain me too,
> And, courteous briars, nail me through.

I was here as in a lonely temple. Snug fire-sides— the low-built roof—parlours ten feet by ten—frugal boards, and all the homeliness of home—these were the condition of my birth—the wholesome soil which I was planted in. Yet, without impeachment to their tenderest lessons, I am not sorry to have had glances of something beyond, and to have taken, if but a peep, in childhood, at the contrasting accidents of a great fortune.

To have the feeling of gentility, it is not necessary to have been born gentle. The pride of ancestry may be had on cheaper terms than to be obliged to an importunate race of ancestors ; and the coatless antiquary in his unemblazoned cell, revolving the long

line of a Mowbray's or De Clifford's pedigree, at those
sounding names may warm himself into as gay a
vanity as those who do inherit them. The claims of
birth are ideal merely, and what herald shall go about
to strip me of an idea ? Is it trenchant to their
swords ? can it be hacked off as a spur can ? or
torn away like a tarnished garter ?

What, else, were the families of the great to us ?
what pleasure should we take in their tedious geneal-
ogies, or their capitulatory brass monuments ? What
to us the uninterrupted current of their bloods, if our
own did not answer within us to a cognate and corresponding elevation ?

Or wherefore, else, O tattered and diminished
'Scutcheon that hung upon the time-worn walls of
thy princely stairs, BLAKESMOOR ! have I in childhood so oft stood poring upon thy mystic characters
—thy emblematic supporters, with their prophetic
" Resurgam "—till, every dreg of peasantry purging
off, I received into myself Very Gentility ? Thou
wert first in my morning eyes ; and of nights hast
detained my steps from bedward, till it was but a
step from gazing at thee to dreaming on thee.

This is the only true gentry by adoption ; the veritable change of blood, and not as empirics have fabled,
by transfusion.

Who it was by dying that had earned the splendid
trophy, I know not, I inquired not ; but its fading
rags, and colours cobweb-stained, told that its subject was of two centuries back.

And what if my ancestor at that date was some
Damœtas,—feeding flocks, not his own, upon the hills
of Lincoln—did I in less earnest vindicate to myself
the family trappings of this once proud Ægon ? re-
paying by a backward triumph the insults he might
possibly have heaped in his life-time upon my poor
pastoral progenitor.

If it were presumption so to speculate, the present

owners of the mansion had least reason to complain. They had long forsaken the old house of their fathers for a newer trifle ; and I was left to appropriate to myself what images I could pick up, to raise my fancy, or to soothe my vanity.

I was the true descendant of those old W——s, and not the present family of that name, who had fled the old waste places.

Mine was that gallery of good old family portraits, which as I have gone over, giving them in fancy my own family name, one—and then another—would seem to smile, reaching forward from the canvas, to recognize the new relationship ; while the rest looked grave, as it seemed, at the vacancy in their dwelling, and thoughts of fled posterity.

The Beauty with the cool blue pastoral drapery, and a lamb—that hung next the great bay window—with the bright yellow H——shire hair, and eye of watchet hue—so like my Alice !—I am persuaded she was a true Elia—Mildred Elia, I take it.

[From her, and from my passion for her—for I first learned love from a picture—Bridget took the hint of those pretty whimsical lines, which thou mayst see, if haply thou hast never seen them, Reader, in the margin. But my Mildred grew not old, like the imaginary Helen.]

Mine, too, BLAKESMOOR, was thy noble Marble Hall, with its mosaic pavements, and its Twelve Cæsars—stately busts in marble—ranged round ; of whose countenances, young reader of faces as I was, the frowning beauty of Nero, I remember, had most of my wonder ; but the mild Galba had my love. There they stood in the coldness of death, yet freshness of immortality.

Mine, too, thy lofty Justice Hall, with its one chair of authority, high-backed and wickered, once the terror of luckless poacher, or self-forgetful maiden— so common since that bats have roosted in it.

Mine, too,—whose else ?—thy costly fruit-garden, with its sun-baked southern wall ; the ampler pleasure garden, rising backwards from the house in triple terraces, with flower-pots now of palest lead, save that a speck here and there, saved from the elements, bespake their pristine state to have been gilt and glittering ; the verdant quarters backwarder still ; and, stretching still beyond, in old formality, thy firry wilderness, the haunt of the squirrel, and the day-long murmuring wood-pigeon, with that antique image in the centre, God or Goddess I wist not ; but child of Athens or old Rome paid never a sincerer worship to Pan or to Sylvanus in their native groves, than I to that fragmental mystery.

Was it for this that I kissed my childish hands too fervently in your idol-worship, walks and windings of BLAKESMOOR ! for this, or what sin of mine, has the plough passed over your pleasant places ? I sometimes think that as men, when they die, do not die all, so of their extinguished habitations there may be a hope—a germ to be revivified.

Old China

I HAVE an almost feminine partiality for old china. When I go to see any great house, I inquire for the china-closet, and next for the picture-gallery. I cannot defend the order of preference, but by saying that we have all some taste or other, of too ancient a date to admit of our remembering distinctly that it was an acquired one. I can call to mind the first play, and the first exhibition, that I was taken to ; but I am not conscious of a time when china jars and saucers were introduced into my imagination.

I had no repugnance then—why should I now have ? —to those little, lawless, azure-tinctured grotesques, that, under the notion of men and women, float about, uncircumscribed by any element, in that world before perspective—a china tea-cup.

I like to see my old friends—whom distance cannot diminish—figuring up in the air (so they appear to our optics), yet on *terra firma* still—for so we must in courtesy interpret that speck of deeper blue, which the decorous artist, to prevent absurdity, had made to spring up beneath their sandals.

I love the men with women's faces, and the women, if possible, with still more womanish expressions.

Here is a young and courtly Mandarin, handing tea to a lady from a salver—two miles off. See how distance seems to set off respect! And here the same lady, or another—for likeness is identity on tea-cups —is stepping into a little fairy boat, moored on the hither side of this calm garden river, with a dainty mincing foot, which in a right angle of incidence (as angles go in our world) must infallibly land her in the midst of a flowery mead—a furlong off on the other side of the same strange stream!

Farther on—if far or near can be predicted of their world—see horses, trees, pagodas, dancing the hays.

Here—a cow and rabbit couchant, and co-extensive —so objects show, seen through the lucid atmosphere of fine Cathay.

I was pointing out to my cousin last evening, over our Hyson (which we are old-fashioned enough to drink unmixed still of an afternoon), some of these *speciosa miracula* upon a set of extraordinary old blue china (a recent purchase) which we were now for the first time using; and could not help remarking, how favourable circumstances had been to us of late years, that we could afford to please the eye sometimes with trifles of this sort—when a passing sentiment seemed to overshade the brows of my companion. I am quick at detecting these summer clouds in Bridget.

"I wish the good old times would come again," she

said, " when we were not quite so rich. I do not mean
that I want to be poor ; but there was a middle state "
—so she was pleased to ramble on,—" in which I am
sure we were a great deal happier. A purchase is but
a purchase, now that you have money enough and to
spare. Formerly it used to be a triumph. When we
coveted a cheap luxury (and, O ! how much ado I
had to get you to consent in those times !)—we
were used to have a debate two or three days before,
and to weigh the *for* and *against*, and think what we
might spare it out of, and what saving we could hit
upon, that should be an equivalent. A thing was
worth buying then, when we felt the money that we
paid for it.

" Do you remember the brown suit, which you
made to hang upon you, till all your friends cried
shame upon you, it grew so threadbare—and all because of that folio Beaumont and Fletcher, which
you dragged home late at night from Barker's in
Covent Garden ? Do you remember how we eyed it
for weeks before we could make up our minds to the
purchase, and had not come to a determination till it
was near ten o'clock of the Saturday night, when you
set off from Islington, fearing you should be too late—
and when the old bookseller with some grumbling
opened his shop, and by the twinkling taper (for he
was setting bedwards) lighted out the relic from his
dusty treasures—and when you lugged it home, wish-
ing it were twice as cumbersome—and when you presented it to me—and when we were exploring the
perfectness of it (*collating*, you called it)—and while
I was repairing some of the loose leaves with paste,
which your impatience would not suffer to be left till
day-break—was there no pleasure in being a poor
man ? or can those neat black clothes which you
wear now, and are so careful to keep brushed, since
we have become rich and finical—give you half the
honest vanity with which you flaunted it about in

that overworn suit—your old corbeau—for four or five weeks longer than you should have done, to pacify your conscience for the mighty sum of fifteen —or sixteen shillings was it?—a great affair we thought it then—which you had lavished on the old folio. Now you can afford to buy any book that pleases you, but I do not see that you ever bring me home any nice old purchases now.

"When you came home with twenty apologies for laying out a less number of shillings upon that print after Lionardo, which we christened the 'Lady Blanch'; when you looked at the purchase, and thought of the money—and thought of the money, and looked again at the picture—was there no pleasure in being a poor man? Now, you have nothing to do but to walk into Colnaghi's, and buy a wilderness of Lionardos. Yet do you?

"Then, do you remember our pleasant walks to Enfield, and Potter's bar, and Waltham, when we had a holyday—holydays and all other fun are gone now we are rich—and the little hand-basket in which I used to deposit our day's fare of savoury cold lamb and salad—and how you would pry about at noontide for some decent house, where we might go in and produce our store—only paying for the ale that you must call for—and speculate upon the looks of the landlady, and whether she was likely to allow us a tablecloth—and wish for such another honest hostess as Izaak Walton has described many a one on the pleasant banks of the Lea, when he went a-fishing—and sometimes they would prove obliging enough, and sometimes they would look grudgingly upon us—but we had cheerful looks still for one another, and would eat our plain food savourily, scarcely grudging Piscator his Trout Hall? Now—when we go out a day's pleasuring, which is seldom, moreover, we *ride* part of the way, and go into a fine inn, and order the best of dinners, never debating the expense—which, after all, never has half the relish of those chance country snaps, when we were at the mercy of uncertain usage, and a precarious welcome.

" You are too proud to see a play anywhere now but in the pit. Do you remember where it was we used to sit, when we saw the battle of Hexham, and the Surrender of Calais, and Bannister and Mrs. Bland in the Children in the Wood—when we squeezed out our shillings a-piece to sit three or four times in a season in the one-shilling gallery—where you felt all the time that you ought not to have brought me— and more strongly I felt obligation to you for having brought me—and the pleasure was the better for a little shame—and when the curtain drew up, what cared we for our place in the house, or what mattered it where we were sitting, when our thoughts were with Rosalind in Arden, or with Viola at the Court of Illyria ? You used to say that the Gallery was the best place of all for enjoying a play socially—that the relish of such exhibitions must be in proportion to the infrequency of going—that the company we met there, not being in general readers of plays, were obliged to attend the more, and did attend to what was going on on the stage—because a word lost would have been a chasm, which it was impossible for them to fill up. With such reflections we consoled our pride then —and I appeal to you whether, as a woman, I met generally with less attention and accommodation than I have done since in more expensive situations in the house ? The getting in, indeed, and the crowding up those inconvenient staircases, was bad enough— but there was still a law of civility to woman recog- nized to quite as great an extent as we ever found in the other passages—and how a little difficulty over- come heightened the snug seat and the play, after- wards ! Now we can only pay our money and walk in. You cannot see, you say, in the galleries now. I am sure we saw, and heard too, well enough then—but sight, and all, I think, is gone with our poverty.

" There was pleasure in eating strawberries, before they became quite common—in the first dish of peas, while they were yet dear—to have them for a nice supper, a treat. What treat can we have now ? If we were to treat ourselves now—that is, to have dainties a little above our means, it would be selfish and wicked. It is the very little more that we allow ourselves beyond what the actual poor can get at, that makes what I call a treat—when two people, living together as we have done, now and then indulge themselves in a cheap luxury, which both like ; while each apologizes, and is willing to take both halves of the blame to his single share. I see no harm in people making much of themselves, in that sense of the word. It may give them a hint how to make much of others. But now—what I mean by the word —we never *do* make much of ourselves. None but the poor can do it. I do not mean the veriest poor of all, but persons as we were, just above poverty.

" I know what you were going to say, that it is mighty pleasant at the end of the year to make all meet,—and much ado we used to have every Thirty-first Night of December to account for our exceedings —many a long face did you make over your puzzled accounts, and in contriving to make it out how we had spent so much—or that we had not spent so much —or that it was impossible we should spend so much next year—and still we found our slender capital decreasing—but then,—betwixt ways, and projects, and compromises of one sort or another, and talk of curtailing this charge, and doing without that for the future—and the hope that youth brings, and laughing spirits (in which you were never poor till now), we pocketed up our loss, and in conclusion, with ' lusty brimmers ' (as you used to quote it out of *hearty cheerful Mr. Cotton*, as you called him), we used to welcome in the ' coming guest.' Now we have no reckoning at all at the end of the old year—no flattering promises about the new year doing better for us."

Bridget is so sparing of her speech on most occasions, that when she gets into a rhetorical vein, I am careful how I interrupt it. I could not help, however, smiling at the phantom of wealth which her dear imagination had conjured up out of a clear income of poor —— hundred pounds a year. " It is true we were happier when we were poorer, but we were also younger, my cousin. I am afraid we must put up with the excess, for if we were to shake the superflux into the sea, we should not much mend ourselves. That we had much to struggle with, as we grew up together, we have reason to be most thankful. It strengthened and knit our compact closer. We could never have been what we have been to each other, if we had always had the sufficiency which you now complain of. The resisting power—those natural dilations of the youthful spirit, which circumstances cannot straiten—with us are long since passed away. Competence to age is supplementary youth, a sorry supplement indeed, but I fear the best that is to be had. We must ride where we formerly walked : live better and lie softer—and shall be wise to do so— than we had means to do in those good old days you speak of. Yet could those days return—could you and I once more walk our thirty miles a day—could Bannister and Mrs. Bland again be young, and you and I be young to see them—could the good old one-shilling gallery days return—they are dreams, my cousin, now—but could you and I at this moment, instead of this quiet argument, by our well-carpeted fireside, sitting on this luxurious sofa—be once more struggling up those inconvenient staircases, pushed about, and squeezed, and elbowed by the poorest rabble of poor gallery scramblers—could I once more hear those anxious shrieks of yours—and the delicious *Thank God, we are safe,* which always followed when the topmost stair, conquered, let in the first light of the whole cheerful theatre down beneath us—I know not the fathom line that ever touched a descent so deep as I would be willing to bury more wealth in than Crœsus had, or the great Jew R—— is supposed to have, to purchase it. And now do just look at that merry little Chinese waiter holding an umbrella, big enough for a bed-tester, over the head of that pretty insipid half Madonna-ish chit of a lady in that very blue summer-house."

1784 — 1859

LEIGH HUNT

25

My Books

SITTING, last winter, among my books, and walled round with all the comfort and protection which they and my fireside could afford me ; to wit, a table of high-piled books at my back, my writing-desk on one side of me, some shelves on the other, and the feeling of the warm fire at my feet ; I began to consider how I loved the authors of those books,—how I loved them, too, not only for the imaginative pleasures they afforded me, but for their making me love the very books themselves, and delight to be in contact with them. I looked sideways at my *Spenser*, my *Theocritus*, and my *Arabian Nights ;* then above them at my Italian poets ; then behind me at my *Dryden* and *Pope*, my romances, and my *Boccaccio ;* then on my left side at my *Chaucer*, who lay on a writing-desk ; and thought how natural it was in C. L. to give a kiss to an old folio, as I once saw him do to *Chapman's Homer*. At the same time I wondered how he could sit in that front room of his with nothing but a few unfeeling tables and chairs, or at best a few engravings in trim frames, instead of putting a couple of arm-chairs into the back-room with the books in it, where there is but one window. Would I were there, with both the chairs properly filled, and one or two more besides ! " We had talk, sir,"—the only talk capable of making one forget the books.

I entrench myself in my books equally against

sorrow and the weather. If the wind comes through a passage, I look about to see how I can fence it off by a better disposition of my movables ; if a melancholy thought is importunate, I give another glance at my *Spenser*. When I speak of being in contact with my books, I mean it literally. I like to lean my head against them. Living in a southern climate, though in a part sufficiently northern to feel the winter, I was obliged, during that season, to take some of the books out of the study, and hang them up near the fireplace in the sitting-room, which is the only room that has such a convenience. I therefore walled myself in, as well as I could, in the manner above mentioned. I took a walk every day, to the astonishment of the Genoese, who used to huddle against a piece of sunny wall, like flies on a chimney-piece ; but I did this only that I might so much the more enjoy my *English* evening. The fire was a wood fire instead of a coal ; but I imagined myself in the country. I remember at the very worst that one end of my native land was not nearer the other than England is to Italy.

While writing this article I am in my study again. Like the rooms in all houses in this country which are not hovels, it is handsome and ornamented. On one side it looks towards a garden and the mountains ; on another to the mountains and the sea. What signifies all this ? I turn my back upon the sea ; I shut up even one of the side windows looking upon the mountains, and retain no prospect but that of the trees. On the right and left of me are book-shelves ; a bookcase is affectionately open in front of me ; and thus kindly enclosed with my books and the green leaves, I write. If all this is too luxurious and effeminate, of all luxuries it is the one that leaves you the most strength. And this is to be said for scholarship in general. It unfits a man for activity, for his bodily part in the world ; but it often doubles both the power and the sense of his mental duties ; and with much indignation against his body, and more against those who tyrannize over the intellectual claims of mankind, the man of letters, like the magician of old, is prepared " to play the devil " with the great men of this world, in a style that astonishes both the sword and the toga.

I do not like this fine large study. I like elegance. I like room to breathe in, and even walk about, when I want to breathe and walk about. I like a great library next my study; but for the study itself, give me a small snug place, almost entirely walled with books. There should be only one window in it, looking upon trees. Some prefer a place with few or no books at all—nothing but a chair or a table, like Epictetus; but I should say that these were philosophers, not lovers of books, if I did not recollect that Montaigne was both. He had a study in a round tower, walled as aforesaid. It is true, one forgets one's books while writing—at least they say so. For my part, I think I have them in a sort of sidelong mind's-eye; like a second thought, which is none—like a waterfall or a whispering wind.

I dislike a grand library to study in. I mean an immense apartment, with books all in Museum order, especially wire-safed. I say nothing against the Museum itself, or public libraries. They are capital places to go to, but not to sit in; and talking of this, I hate to read in public, and in strange company. The jealous silence; the dissatisfied looks of the messengers; the inability to help yourself; the not knowing whether you really ought to trouble the messengers, much less the *gentleman* in black, or brown, who is, perhaps, half a trustee; with a variety of other jarrings between privacy and publicity, prevent one's settling heartily to work. They say " they manage these things better in France; " and I dare say they do; but I think I should feel still more *distrait* in France, in spite of the benevolence of the servitors, and the generous profusion of pen, ink, and paper. I should feel as if I were doing nothing but interchanging amenities with polite writers.

A grand private library, which the master of the house also makes his study, never looks to me like a real place of books, much less of authorship. I cannot take kindly to it. It is certainly not out of envy ; for three parts of the books are generally trash, and I can seldom think of the rest and the proprietor together. It reminds me of a fine gentleman, of a collector, of a patron, of Gil Blas and the Marquis of Marialva ; of anything but genius and comfort. I have a particular hatred of a round table (not *the* Round Table, for that was a dining one) covered and irradiated with books, and never met with one in the house of a clever man but once. It is the reverse of Montaigne's Round Tower. Instead of bringing the books around you, they all seem turning another way, and eluding your hands.

Conscious of my propriety and comfort in these matters, I take an interest in the bookcases as well as the books of my friends. I long to meddle and dispose them after my own notions. When they see this confession, they will acknowledge the virtue I have practised. I believe I did mention his book-room to C. L., and I think he told me that he often sat there when alone. It would be hard not to believe him. His library, though not abounding in Greek or Latin (which are the only things to help some persons to an idea of literature), is anything but superficial. The depth of philosophy and poetry are there, the innermost passages of the human heart. It has some Latin too. It has also a handsome contempt for appearance. It looks like what it is, a selection made at precious intervals from the book-stalls ;—now a Chaucer at nine and twopence ; now a Montaigne or a Sir Thomas Browne at two shillings ; now a Jeremy Taylor ; a Spinoza ; an old English Dramatist, Prior, and Sir Philip Sidney ; and the books are " neat as imported."

The very perusal of the backs is a "discipline of humanity." There Mr. Southey takes his place again with an old Radical friend : there Jeremy Collier is at peace with Dryden : there the lion, Martin Luther, lies down with the Quaker lamb, Sewell : there Guzman d'Alfarache thinks himself fit company for Sir Charles Grandison, and has his claims admitted. Even the "high fantastical" Duchess of Newcastle, with her laurel on her head, is received with grave honours, and not the less for declining to trouble herself with the constitutions of her maids. There is an approach to this in the library of W. C., who also includes Italian among his humanities. W. H., I believe, has no books except mine ; but he has Shakespeare and Rousseau by heart. N., who, though not a book-man by profession, is fond of those who are, and who loves his volume enough to read it across the fields, has his library in the common sitting-room, which is hospitable. H. R.'s books are all too modern and finely bound, which, however, is not his fault, for they were left him by will,—not the most kindly act of the testator. Suppose a man were to bequeath us a great japan chest three feet by four, with an injunction that it was always to stand on the tea-table. I remember borrowing a book of H. R., which, having lost, I replaced with a copy equally well bound. I am not sure I should have been in such a haste, even to return the book, had it been a common-looking volume ; but the splendour of the loss dazzled me into this ostentatious piece of propriety. I set about restoring it as if I had diminished his fortunes, and waived the privilege a friend has to use a man's things as his own. I may venture upon this ultra-liberal theory, not only because candour compels me to say that I hold it to it to a greater extent, with Montaigne, but because I have been a meek son in the family of book-losers. I may affirm, upon a moderate calculation, that I have lent and lost in my time (and I am eight-and-thirty,)

half a dozen decent-sized libraries,—I mean books
enough to fill so many ordinary bookcases. I have
never complained ; and self-love, as well as gratitude,
makes me love those who do not complain of me.

I own I borrow books with as much facility as I
lend. I cannot see a work that interests me on
another person's shelf, without a wish to carry it off ;
but, I repeat, that I have been much more sinned
against than sinning in the article of non-return ; and
am scrupulous in the article of intention. I never had
a felonious intent upon a book but once ; and then I
shall only say, it was under circumstances so peculiar,
that I cannot but look upon the conscience that induced me to restore it, as having sacrificed the spirit
of its very self to the letter ; and I have a grudge
against it accordingly. Some people are unwilling to
lend their books. I have a special grudge against
them, particularly those who accompany their un-
willingness with uneasy professions to the contrary,
and smiles like Sir Fretful Plagiary. The friend who
helped to spoil my notions of property, or rather to
make them too good for the world " as it goes," taught
me also to undervalue my squeamishness in refusing
to avail myself of the books of these gentlemen. He
showed me how it was doing good to all parties to put
an ordinary face on the matter ; though I know his
own blushed not a little sometimes in doing it, even
when the good to be done was for another. I feel, in
truth, that even when anger inclines me to exercise
this privilege of philosophy, it is more out of revenge
than contempt. I fear that in allowing myself to
borrow books, I sometimes make extremes meet in a
very sinful manner, and do it out of a refined revenge.
It is like eating a miser's beef at him.

I yield to none in my love of bookstall urbanity. I
have spent as happy moments over the stalls as any
literary apprentice boy who ought to be moving on-
wards. But I confess my weakness in liking to see

some of my favourite purchases neatly bound. The books I like to have about me most are—Spenser, Chaucer, the minor poems of Milton, the *Arabian Nights*, Theocritus, Ariosto, and such old good-natured speculations as Plutarch's *Morals*. For most of these I like a plain, good, old binding, never mind how old, provided it wears well ; but my *Arabian Nights* may be bound in as fine and flowery a style as possible, and I should love an engraving to every dozen pages. Book-prints of all sorts, bad and good, take with me as much as when I was a child ; and I think some books, such as Prior's Poems, ought always to have portraits of the authors. Prior's airy face with his cap on is like having his company. From early association, no edition of Milton pleases me so much as that in which there are pictures of the Devil with brute ears, dressed like a Roman General : nor of Bunyan, as the one containing the print of the Valley of the Shadow of Death, with the Devil whispering in Christian's ear, or old Pope by the wayside, and

> " Vanity Fair,
> With the Pilgrims suffering there."

I delight in the recollection of the puzzle I used to have with the frontispiece of the *Tale of a Tub*, of my real horror at the sight of that crawling old man, representing Avarice, at the beginning of *Enfield's Speaker*, the *Looking-Glass*, or some such book ; and even of the careless school-boy hats, and the prim stomachers and cottage bonnets, of such golden-age antiquities as the *Village School*. The oldest and most worn-out woodcut, representing King Pippin, Goody Two Shoes, or the grim Soldan, sitting with three staring blots for his eyes and mouth, his sceptre in one hand, and his other five fingers raised and spread in admiration at the feats of the Gallant London 'Prentice, cannot excite in me a feeling of ingratitude. Cooke's edition of the

British Poets and Novelists came out when I was at school : for which reason I never could put up with Suttaby's or Walker's publications, except in the case of such works as the *Fairy Tales*, which Mr. Cooke did not publish. Besides, they are too cramped, thick, and mercenary ; and the pictures are all frontispieces. They do not come in at the proper places. Cooke realized the old woman's *beau idéal* of a prayer-book, —" A little book, with a great deal of matter, and a large type : "—for the type was really large for so small a volume. Shall I ever forget his Collins and his Gray, books at once so " superbly ornamented " and so inconceivably cheap ? Sixpence could procure much before ; but never could it procure so much as then, or was at once so much respected, and so little cared for. His artist Kirk was the best artist, except Stothard, that ever designed for periodical works ; and I will venture to add (if his name rightly announces his country) the best artist Scotland ever produced, except Wilkie, but he unfortunately had not enough of his country in him to keep him from dying young. His designs for Milton and the *Arabian Nights*, his female extricated from the water in the *Tales of the Genii*, and his old hag issuing out of the chest of the Merchant Abadah in the same book, are before me now, as vividly as they were then. He possessed elegance and the sense of beauty in no ordinary degree ; though they sometimes played a trick or so of foppery. I shall never forget the gratitude with which I received an odd number of Akenside, value sixpence, one of the set of that poet, which a boarder distributed among three or four of us, " with his mother's compliments." The present might have been more lavish, but I hardly thought of that. I remember my number. It was the one in which there is a picture of the poet on a sofa, with Cupid coming to him, and the words underneath, " Tempt me no more, insidious love ! " The picture and the number appeared to me equally divine. I cannot help thinking to this day, that it is right and natural in a gentleman to sit in a stage dress, on that particular kind of sofa, though on no other, with that exclusive hat and feathers on his head, telling Cupid to begone with a tragic air.

I love an author the more for having been himself a lover of books. The idea of an ancient library perplexes our sympathy by its map-like volumes, rolled upon cylinders. Our imagination cannot take kindly to a yard of wit, or to thirty inches of moral observation, rolled out like linen in a draper's shop. But we conceive of Plato as of a lover of books ; of Aristotle certainly ; of Plutarch, Pliny, Horace, Julian, and Marcus Aurelius. Virgil, too, must have been one ; and, after a fashion, Martial. May I confess, that the passage which I recollect with the greatest pleasure in Cicero, is where he says that books delight us at home, *and are no impediment abroad ;* travel with us, ruralize with us. His period is rounded off to some purpose : " *Delectant domi, non impediunt foris ; peregrinantur, rusticantur.*" I am so much of this opinion that I do not care to be anywhere without having a book or books at hand, and like Dr. Orkborne, in the novel of *Camilla,* stuff the coach or post-chaise with them whenever I travel. As books, however, become ancient, the love of them becomes more unequivocal and conspicuous. The ancients had little of what we call learning. They made it. They were also no very eminent buyers of books—they made books for posterity. It is true, that it is not at all necessary to love many books, in order to love them much. The scholar, in Chaucer, who would rather have

> " At his beddes head
> A twenty bokes, clothed, in black and red,
> Of Aristotle and his philosophy,
> Than robès rich, or fiddle, or psaltrie,—"

doubtless beat all our modern collectors in his passion for reading ; but books must at least exist, and have acquired an eminence, before their lovers can make themselves known.   There must be a possession, also, to perfect the communion ; and the mere contact is much, even when our mistress speaks an unknown language.   Dante puts Homer, the great ancient, in his *Elysium* upon trust ; but a few years afterwards, *Homer*, the book, made its appearance in Italy, and Petrarch, in a transport, put it upon his book-shelves, where he adored it, like " the unknown God."   Petrarch ought to be the god of the bibliomaniacs, for he was a collector and a man of genius, which is a union that does not often happen.   He copied out, with his own precious hand, the manuscripts he rescued from time, and then produced others for time to reverence. With his head upon a book he died.   Boccaccio, his friend, was another ; nor can one look upon the longest and most tiresome works he wrote (for he did write some tiresome ones, in spite of the gaiety of his *Decameron*), without thinking, that in that resuscitation of the world of letters it must have been natural to a man of genius to add to the existing stock of volumes, at whatsoever price.   I always pitch my completest idea of a lover of books, either in those dark ages, as they are called,

" Cui cieco a torto il cieco volgo appella—"

or in the gay town days of Charles II., or a little afterwards.   In both times the portrait comes out by the force of contrast.   In the first, I imagine an age of iron warfare and energy, with solitary retreats, in which the monk or the hooded scholar walks forth to meditate, his precious volume under his arm.   In the other, I have a triumphant example of the power of books and wit to contest the victory with sensual pleasure :—Rochester, staggering home to pen a satire in the style of Monsieur Boileau ; Butler, cramming his jolly duodecimo with all the learning that he laughed at ; and a new race of book poets come up, who, in spite of their periwigs and petit-maîtres, talk as romantically of " the bays," as if they were priests of Delphos. It was a victorious thing in books to beguile even the old French of their egotism, or at least to share it with them. Nature never pretended to do as much. And here is the difference between the two ages, or between any two ages in which genius and art predominate. In the one, books are loved because they are the records of Nature and her energies ; in the other, because they are the records of those records, or evidences of the importance of the individuals, and proofs of our descent in the new imperishable aristocracy. This is the reason why rank (with few exceptions) is so jealous of literature, and loves to appropriate or withhold the honours of it, as if they were so many toys and ribbons, like its own. It has an instinct that the two pretensions are incompatible. When Montaigne (a real lover of books) affected the order of St. Michael, and pleased himself with possessing that fugitive little piece of importance, he did it because he would pretend to be above nothing that he really felt, or that was felt by men in general ; but at the same time he vindicated his natural superiority over this weakness by praising and loving all higher and lasting things, and by placing his best glory in doing homage to the geniuses that had gone before him. He did not endeavour to think that an immortal renown was a fashion, like that of the cut of his scarf ; or that by undervaluing the one, he should go shining down to posterity in the other, perpetual lord of Montaigne and of the ascendant.

There is a period of modern times, at which the love of books appears to have been of a more decided nature than at either of these—I mean the age just before and after the Reformation, or rather all that period when book-writing was confined to the learned languages. Erasmus is the god of it. Bacon, a mighty bookman, saw, among his other sights, the great advantage of loosening the vernacular tongue, and wrote both Latin and English. I allow this is the greatest closeted age of books ; of old scholars sitting in dusty studies ; of heaps of " illustrious obscure," rendering themselves more illustrious and more obscure by retreating from the " thorny queaches " of Dutch and German names into the " vacant interlunar caves " of appellations latinized or translated. I think I see all their volumes now, filling the shelves of a dozen German convents. The authors are bearded men, sitting in old woodcuts, in caps and gowns, and their books are dedicated to princes and statesmen, as illustrious as themselves. My old friend Wierus, who wrote a thick book, *De Præstigiis Dæmonum*, was one of them, and had a fancy worthy of his sedentary stomach. I will confess, once for all, that I have a liking for them all. It is my link with the bibliomaniacs, whom I admit into our relationship, because my love is large, and my family pride nothing. But still I take my idea of books read with a gusto, of companions for bed and board, from the two ages before mentioned. The other is of too bookworm a description. There must be both a judgment and a fervour ; a discrimination and a boyish eagerness ; and (with all due humility) something of a point of contact between authors worth reading and the reader. How can I take Juvenal into the fields, or Valcarenghius' *De Aortæ Aneurismate* to bed with me ? How could I expect to walk before the face of nature with the one ; to tire my elbow properly with the other, before I put out my candle, and turn round deliciously on the right side ? Or how could I stick up Coke upon Littleton against something on the dinner-table, and be divided between a fresh paragraph and a mouthful of salad ?

I take our four great English poets to have all been

fond of reading. Milton and Chaucer proclaim themselves for hard sitters at books. Spenser's reading is evident by his learning ; and if there was nothing else to show for it in Shakespeare, his retiring to his native town, long before old age, would be a proof of it. It is impossible for a man to live in solitude without such assistance, unless he is a metaphysician or mathematician, or the dullest of mankind ; and any country town would be solitude to Shakespeare, after the bustle of a metropolis and a theatre. Doubtless he divided his time between his books, and his bowling-green, and his daughter Susanna. It is pretty certain, also, that he planted, and rode on horseback ; and there is evidence of all sorts to make it clear, that he must have occasionally joked with the blacksmith, and stood godfather for his neighbours' children. Chaucer's account of himself must be quoted, for the delight and sympathy of all true readers :—

> " And as for me, though that I can but lite,
>   On bookès for to rede I me delite,
>   And to hem yeve I faith and full credènce,
>   And in mine herte have hem in reverence
>   So hertèly, that there is gamè none,
>   That fro my bookès maketh me to gone,
>   But it is seldome on the holy daie ;
>   Save certainly whan that the month of May
>   Is comen, and that I hear the foulès sing,
>   And that the flourès ginnen for to spring.
>   Farewell my booke and my dovociön."
>   *The Legend of Good Women.*

And again, in the second book of his *House of Fame*, where *the eagle* addresses him :—

> " ———Thou wilt make
>   At night full oft thine head to ake,
>   And in thy study as thou writest,
>   And evermore of Love enditest.

> In honour of him and his praisings,
> And in his folkès furtherings,
> And in his matter all devisest,
> And not him ne his folke despisest,
> Although thou mayest go in the daunse
> Of hem, that him list not advance,
> Therefore as I said, ywis,
> Jupiter considreth well this.
> And also, beausire, of other things ;
> That is, thou hast no tidings
> Of Lovès folke, if they be glade,
> Ne of nothing else that God made,
> And not only fro ferre countree,
> But no tidings commen to thee,
> Not of thy very neighbouris,
> That dwellen almost at thy dores ;
> Thou hearest neither that ne this,
> For whan thy labour all done is,
> And hast made all thy rekenings,
> Instead of rest and of new things,
> Thou goest home to thine house anone,
> And all so dombe as anie stone,
> Thou sittest at another booke,
> Till fully dazed is thy looke."

After I think of the bookishness of Chaucer and Milton, I always make a great leap to Prior and Fenton. Prior was first noticed, when a boy, by Lord Dorset, sitting in his uncle's tavern, and reading Horace. He describes himself, years after, when Secretary of Embassy at the Hague, as taking the same author with him in the Saturday's chaise, in which he and his mistress used to escape from town cares into the country, to the admiration of Dutch beholders. Fenton was a martyr to contented scholarship (including a sirloin and a bottle of wine), and died among his books, of inactivity. "He rose late," says Johnson, "and when he had risen, sat down to his books and papers." A woman that once waited on him in a lodging, told him, as she said, that he would " lie a-bed and be fed with a spoon." He must have had an enviable liver, if he was happy. I must own (if my conscience would let me), that I should like to lead, half the year, just such a life (woman included, though not that woman), the other half being passed in the fields and woods, with a cottage just big enough to hold us. Dacier and his wife had a pleasant time of it ; both fond of books, both scholars, both amiable, both wrapt up in the ancient world, and helping one another at their tasks. If they were not happy, matrimony would be a rule even without an exception. Pope does not strike me as being a bookman ; he was curious rather than enthusiastic ; more nice than wise ; he dabbled in modern Latin poetry, which is a bad symptom. Swift was decidedly a reader ; the *Tale of a Tub*, in its fashion as well as substance, is the work of a scholarly wit ; the *Battle of Books* is the fancy of a lover of libraries. Addison and Steele were too much given up to Button's and the town. Periodical writing, though its demands seem otherwise, is not favourable to reading ; it becomes too much a matter of business, and will either be attended to at the expense of the writer's books, or books, the very admonishers of his industry, will make him idle. Besides, a periodical work, to be suitable to its character, and warrant its regular recurrence, must involve something of a gossiping nature, and proceed upon experiences familiar to the existing community, or at least likely to be received by them in consequence of some previous tinge of inclination. You do not pay weekly visits to your friends to lecture them, whatever good you may do their minds. There will be something compulsory in reading the *Ramblers*, as there is in going to church. Addison and Steele undertook to regulate the minor morals of society, and effected a world of good, with which scholarship had little to do. Gray was a bookman ; he wished to be always lying on sofas, reading " eternal new novels of Crebillon and Marivaux." This is a true hand. The elaborate and

scientific look of the rest of his reading was owing to
the necessity of employing himself : he had not health
and spirits for the literary voluptuousness he desired.
Collins, for the same reason, could not employ himself ; he was obliged to dream over Arabian tales, to
let the light of the supernatural world half in upon his
eyes. " He loved," as Johnson says (in that strain of
music, inspired by tenderness), " fairies, genii, giants,
and monsters ; he delighted to rove through the
meanders of enchantment, to gaze on the magnificence
of golden palaces, to repose by the waterfalls of
Elysian gardens." If Collins had had a better constitution, I do not believe that he would have written
his projected work upon the *Restoration of Literature*,
fit as he was by scholarship for the task, but he would
have been the greatest poet since the days of Milton.
If his friend Thomas Warton had had a little more of
his delicacy of organization, the love of books would
almost have made him a poet. His edition of the
minor poems of Milton is a wilderness of sweets. It is
the only one in which a true lover of the original can
pardon an exuberance of annotation ; though I confess I am inclined enough to pardon any notes that
resemble it, however numerous. The " builded
rhyme " stands at the top of the page, like a fair
edifice, with all sorts of flowers and fresh waters at its
foot. The young poet lives there, served by the
nymphs and fauns.

> " Hinc atque hinc glomerantur Oreades.
>   Huc ades, o formose puer ; tibi lilia plenis
>   Ecce ferunt nymphæ calathis : tibi candida Nais
>   Pallentes violas et summa papavera carpens,
>   Narcissum et florem jungit bene olentis anethi."

Among the old writers I must not forget Ben Jonson
and Donne. Cowley has been already mentioned. His
boyish love of books, like all the other inclinations of
his early life, stuck to him to the last, which is the

greatest reward of virtue. I would mention Izaak Walton, if I had not a grudge against him. His brother fishermen, the divines, were also great fishers of books. I have a grudge against them and their divinity. They talked much of the devil and divine right, and yet forgot what Shakespeare says of the devil's friend Nero, that he is " an angler in the lake of darkness." Selden was called " the walking library of our nation." It is not the pleasantest idea of him ; but the library included poetry, and wit, as well as heraldry and the Jewish doctors. His *Table Talk* is equally pithy and pleasant, and truly worthy of the name, for it implies other speakers. Indeed, it was actually what it is called, and treasured up by his friends. Selden wrote complimentary verses to his friends the poets, and a commentary on Drayton's *Polyolbion.* Drayton was himself a reader, addicted to all the luxuries of scholarship. Chapman sat among his books, like an astrologer among his spheres and altitudes.

How pleasant it is to reflect, that all those lovers of books have themselves become books ! What better metamorphosis could Pythagoras have desired ? How Ovid and Horace exulted in anticipating theirs ! And how the world have justified their exultation ! They had a right to triumph over brass and marble. It is the only visible change which changes no farther ; which generates and yet is not destroyed. Consider : mines themselves are exhausted ; cities perish ; kingdoms are swept away, and man weeps with indignation to think that his own body is not immortal.

> " Muoiono le città, muoiono i regni,
> E l' uom d' esser mortal par che si sdegni."

Yet this little body of thought, that lies before me in the shape of a book, has existed thousands of years, nor since the invention of the press can anything short of an universal convulsion of nature abolish it. To a shape like this, so small yet so comprehensive, so slight yet so lasting, so insignificant yet so venerable, turns the mighty activity of Homer, and so turning, is enabled to live and warm us for ever. To a shape like this turns the placid sage of Academus : to a shape like this the grandeur of Milton, the exuberance of Spenser, the pungent elegance of Pope, and the volatility of Prior. In one small room, like the compressed spirits of Milton, can be gathered together

"The assembled souls of all that men held wise."

May I hope to become the meanest of these existences? This is a question which every author who is a lover of books asks himself some time in his life ; and which must be pardoned, because it cannot be helped. I know not. I cannot exclaim with the poet,

"Oh that my name were number'd among theirs,
  Then gladly would I end my mortal days."

For my mortal days, few and feeble as the rest of them may be, are of consequence to others. But I should like to remain visible in this shape. The little of myself that pleases myself, I could wish to be accounted worth pleasing others. I should like to survive so, were it only for the sake of those who love me in private, knowing as I do what a treasure is the possession of a friend's mind when he is no more. At all events, nothing while I live and think can deprive me of my value for such treasures. I can help the appreciation of them while I last, and love them till I die ; and perhaps, if fortune turns her face once more in kindness upon me before I go, I may chance, some quiet day, to lay my overbeating temples on a book, and so have the death I most envy.

WILLIAM HAZLITT 1778-1430

On Going a Journey

ONE of the pleasantest things in the world is going a journey; but I like to go by myself. I can enjoy society in a room; but out of doors, nature is company enough for me. I am then never less alone than when alone.

> "The fields his study, nature was his book."

I cannot see the wit of walking and talking at the same time. When I am in the country I wish to vegetate like the country. I am not for criticizing hedgerows and black cattle. I go out of town in order to forget the town and all that is in it. There are those who for this purpose go to watering-places, and carry the metropolis with them. I like more elbow-room and fewer encumbrances. I like solitude, when I give myself up to it, for the sake of solitude; nor do I ask for

> "a friend in my retreat,
> Whom I may whisper solitude is sweet."

The soul of a journey is liberty, perfect liberty, to think, feel, do just as one pleases. We go a journey chiefly to be free of all impediments and of all inconveniences; to leave ourselves behind, much more to get rid of others. It is because I want a little breathing-space to muse on indifferent matters, where Contemplation

> " May plume her feathers and let grow her wings,
>   That in the various bustle of resort
>   Were all too ruffled, and sometimes impair'd,"

that I absent myself from the town for a while, without feeling at a loss the moment I am left by myself. Instead of a friend in a post-chaise or in a tilbury, to exchange good things with, and vary the same stale topics over again, for once let me have a truce with impertinence. Give me the clear blue sky over my head, and the green turf beneath my feet, a winding road before me, and a three hours' march to dinner—and then to thinking ! It is hard if I cannot start some game on these lone heaths. I laugh, I run, I leap, I sing for joy. From the point of yonder rolling cloud I plunge into my past being, and revel there, as the sun-burnt Indian plunges headlong into the wave that wafts him to his native shore. Then long-forgotten things, like " sunken wrack and sumless treasuries," burst upon my eager sight, and I begin to feel, think, and be myself again. Instead of an awkward silence, broken by attempts at wit or dull common-places, mine is that undisturbed silence of the heart which alone is perfect eloquence. No one likes puns, alliterations, antitheses, argument, and analysis better than I do ; but I sometimes had rather be without them. " Leave, oh, leave me to my repose ! " I have just now other business in hand, which would seem idle to you, but is with me " very stuff o' the conscience." Is not this wild rose sweet without a comment ? Does not this daisy leap to my heart set in its coat of emerald ? Yet if I were to explain to you the circumstance that has so endeared it to me, you would only smile. Had I not better then keep it to myself, and let it serve me to brood over, from here to yonder craggy point, and from thence

onward to the far-distant horizon ? I should be but
bad company all that way, and therefore prefer being
alone. I have heard it said that you may, when the
moody fit comes on, walk or ride on by yourself, and
indulge your reveries. But this looks like a breach
of manners, a neglect of others, and you are thinking
all the time that you ought to rejoin your party.
" Out upon such half-faced fellowship," say I. I like
to be either entirely to myself, or entirely at the dis-
posal of others ; to talk or be silent, to walk or sit
still, to be sociable or solitary. I was pleased with an
observation of Mr. Cobbett's, that " he thought it a
bad French custom to drink our wine with our meals,
and that an Englishman ought to do only one thing
at a time." So I cannot talk and think, or indulge in
melancholy musing and lively conversation by fits
and starts. " Let me have a companion of my way,"
says Sterne, " were it but to remark how the shadows
lengthen as the sun declines." It is beautifully said ;
but, in my opinion, this continual comparing of notes
interferes with the involuntary impression of things
upon the mind, and hurts the sentiment. If you only
hint what you feel in a kind of dumb show, it is insipid : if you have to explain it, it is making a toil of
a pleasure. You cannot read the book of nature without being perpetually put to the trouble of translating
it for the benefit of others. I am for the synthetical
method on a journey in preference to the analytical.
I am content to lay in a stock of ideas then, and to
examine and anatomize them afterwards. I want to
see my vague notions float like the down of the thistle
before the breeze, and not to have them entangled in
the briars and thorns of controversy. For once, I like
to have it all my own way ; and this is impossible
unless you are alone, or in such company as I do not
covet. I have no objection to argue a point with any
one for twenty miles of measured road, but not for
pleasure. If you remark the scent of a bean-field

crossing the road, perhaps your fellow-traveller has no smell. If you point to a distant object, perhaps he is short-sighted, and has to take out his glass to look at it. There is a feeling in the air, a tone in the colour of a cloud, which hits your fancy, but the effect of which you are unable to account for. There is then no sympathy, but an uneasy craving after it, and a dissatisfaction which pursues you on the way, and in the end probably produces ill-humour. Now I never quarrel with myself, and take all my own conclusions for granted till I find it necessary to defend them against objections. It is not merely that you may not be of accord on the objects and circumstances that present themselves before you—these may recall a number of objects, and lead to associations too delicate and refined to be possibly communicated to others. Yet these I love to cherish, and sometimes still fondly clutch them, when I can escape from the throng to do so. To give way to our feelings before company seems extravagance or affectation ; and, on the other hand, to have to unravel this mystery of our being at every turn, and to make others take an equal interest in it (otherwise the end is not answered), is a task to which few are competent. We must " give it an understanding, but no tongue." My old friend Coleridge, however, could do both. He could go on in the most delightful explanatory way over hill and dale, a summer's day, and convert a landscape into a didactic poem or a Pindaric ode. " He talked far above singing." If I could so clothe my ideas in sounding and flowing words, I might perhaps wish to have some one with me to admire the swelling theme; or I could be more content, were it possible for me still to hear his echoing voice in the woods of All-Foxden. They had " that fine madness in them which our first poets had " ; and if they could have been caught by some rare instrument, would have breathed such strains as the following :

" Here be woods as green
As any, air likewise as fresh and sweet
As when smooth Zephyrus plays on the fleet
Face of the curled stream, with flow'rs as many
As the young spring gives, and as choice as any ;
Here be all new delights, cool streams and wells,
Arbours o'ergrown with woodbines, caves and dells ;
Choose where thou wilt, whilst I sit by and sing,
Or gather rushes to make many a ring
For thy long fingers ; tell thee tales of love,
How the pale Phœbe, hunting in a grove,
First saw the boy Endymion, from whose eyes
She took eternal fire that never dies ;
How she convey'd him softly in a sleep,
His temples bound with poppy, to the steep
Head of old Latmos, where she stoops each night,
Gilding the mountain with her brother's light,
To kiss her sweetest."

Had I words and images at command like these, I
would attempt to wake the thoughts that lie slumber-
ing on golden ridges in the evening clouds : but at the
sight of nature my fancy, poor as it is, droops and
closes up its leaves, like flowers at sunset. I can make
nothing out on the spot : I must have time to collect
myself.

In general, a good thing spoils out-of-door prospects:
it should be reserved for Table-talk. Lamb is for this
reason, I take it, the worst company in the world out
of doors ; because he is the best within. I grant there
is one subject on which it is pleasant to talk on a
journey, and that is, what one shall have for supper
when we get to our inn at night. The open air im-
proves this sort of conversation or friendly altercation,
by setting a keener edge on appetite. Every mile of
the road heightens the flavour of the viands we expect
at the end of it. How fine it is to enter some old
town, walled and turreted, just at approach of night-
fall, or to come to some straggling village, with the
lights streaming through the surrounding gloom ; and

then, after inquiring for the best entertainment that
the place affords, to " take one's ease at one's inn ! "
These eventful moments in our lives' history are too
precious, too full of solid, heartfelt happiness to be
frittered and dribbled away in imperfect sympathy. I
would have them all to myself, and drain them to the
last drop : they will do to talk of or to write about
afterwards. What a delicate speculation it is, after
drinking whole goblets of tea—

" The cups that cheer, but not inebriate— "

and letting the fumes ascend into the brain, to sit
considering what we shall have for supper—eggs and a
rasher, a rabbit smothered in onions, or an excellent
veal cutlet ! Sancho in such a situation once fixed on
cow-heel ; and his choice, though he could not help
it, is not to be disparaged. Then, in the intervals
of pictured scenery and Shandean contemplation, to
catch the preparation and the stir in the kitchen
[getting ready for the gentlemen in the parlour].
Procul, O procul este profani ! These hours are sacred
to silence and to musing, to be treasured up in the
memory, and to feed the source of smiling thoughts
hereafter. I would not waste them in idle talk ; or if
I must have the integrity of fancy broken in upon, I
would rather it were by a stranger than a friend. A
stranger takes his hue and character from the time
and place ; he is a part of the furniture and costume
of an inn. If he is a Quaker, or from the West Riding
of Yorkshire, so much the better. I do not even try
to sympathize with him, and he breaks no squares.
[How I love to see the camps of the gypsies, and to
sigh my soul into that sort of life. If I express this
feeling to another, he may qualify and spoil it with
some objection.] I associate nothing with my travelling companion but present objects and passing events.
In his ignorance of me and my affairs, I in a manner

forget myself. But a friend reminds one of other things, rips up old grievances, and destroys the abstraction of the scene. He comes in ungraciously between us and our imaginary character. Something is dropped in the course of conversation that gives a hint of your profession and pursuits ; or from having some one with you that knows the less sublime portions of your history, it seems that other people do. You are no longer a citizen of the world ; but your " unhoused free condition is put into circumspection and confine." The incognito of an inn is one of its striking privileges—" lord of one's self, uncumbered with a name." Oh ! it is great to shake off the trammels of the world and of public opinion—to lose our importunate, tormenting, everlasting personal identity in the elements of nature, and become the creature of the moment, clear of all ties—to hold to the universe only by a dish of sweetbreads, and to owe nothing but the score of the evening—and no longer seeking for applause and meeting with contempt, to be known by no other title than *the Gentleman in the parlour !* One may take one's choice of all characters in this romantic state of uncertainty as to one's real pretensions, and become indefinitely respectable and negatively right worshipful. We baffle prejudice and disappoint conjecture ; and from being so to others, begin to be objects of curiosity and wonder even to ourselves. We are no more those hackneyed common-places that we appear in the world ; an inn restores us to the level of nature, and quits scores with society ! I have certainly spent some enviable hours at inns—sometimes when I have been left entirely to myself, and have tried to solve some metaphysical problem, as once at Witham Common, where I found out the proof that likeness is not a case of the association of ideas—at other times, when there have been pictures in the room, as at St. Neot's (I think it was), where I first met with Gribelin's engravings of the Cartoons, into

which I entered at once, and at a little inn on the
borders of Wales, where there happened to be hanging
some of Westall's drawings, which I compared trium-
phantly (for a theory that I had, not for the admired
artist) with the figure of a girl who had ferried me over
the Severn, standing up in a boat between me and the
twilight—at other times I might mention luxuriating
in books, with a peculiar interest in this way, as I remember sitting up half the night to read *Paul and
Virginia*, which I picked up at an inn at Bridgewater,
after being drenched in the rain all day; and at the
same place I got through two volumes of Madame
d'Arblay's *Camilla*. It was on the 10th of April 1798
that I sat down to a volume of the *New Eloise*, at the
inn at Llangollen, over a bottle of sherry and a cold
chicken. The letter I chose was that in which St.
Preux describes his feelings as he first caught a glimpse
from the heights of the Jura of the Pays de Vaud,
which I had brought with me as a *bon bouche* to crown
the evening with. It was my birthday, and I had for
the first time come from a place in the neighbourhood
to visit this delightful spot. The road to Llangollen
turns off between Chirk and Wrexham; and on passing a certain point you come all at once upon the
valley, which opens like an amphitheatre, broad,
barren hills rising in majestic state on either side, with
" green upland swells that echo to the bleat of flocks "
below, and the river Dee babbling over its stony bed
in the midst of them. The valley at this time " glit-
tered green with sunny showers," and a budding ash-
tree dipped its tender branches in the chiding stream.
How proud, how glad I was to walk along the high
road that overlooks the delicious prospect, repeating
the lines which I have just quoted from Mr. Coleridge's
poems! But besides the prospect which opened
beneath my feet, another also opened to my inward
sight, a heavenly vision, on which were written, in
letters large as Hope could make them, these four

words, LIBERTY, GENIUS, LOVE, VIRTUE ; which have since faded into the light of common day, or mock my idle gaze.

" The beautiful is vanished, and returns not."

Still I would return some time or other to this enchanted spot ; but I would return to it alone. What other self could I find to share that influx of thoughts, of regret and delight, the fragments of which I could hardly conjure up to myself, so much have they been broken and defaced. I could stand on some tall rock, and overlook the precipice of years that separates me from what I then was. I was at that time going shortly to visit the poet whom I have above named. Where is he now ? Not only I myself have changed ; the world, which was then new to me, has become old and incorrigible. Yet will I turn to thee in thought, O sylvan Dee, in joy, in youth and gladness as thou then wert ; and thou shalt always be to me the river of Paradise, where I will drink of the waters of life freely !

There is hardly anything that shows the shortsightedness or capriciousness of the imagination more than travelling does. With change of place we change our ideas ; nay, our opinions and feelings. We can by an effort indeed transport ourselves to old and long-forgotten scenes, and then the picture of the mind revives again ; but we forget those that we have just left. It seems that we can think but of one place at a time. The canvas of the fancy is but of a certain extent, and if we paint one set of objects upon it, they immediately efface every other. We cannot enlarge our conceptions, we only shift our point of view. The landscape bares its bosom to the enraptured eye, we take our fill of it, and seem as if we could form no other image of beauty or grandeur. We pass on, and think no more of it : the horizon that shuts it from our sight also blots it from our memory like a dream. In travelling through a wild barren country I can form no idea of a woody and cultivated one. It appears to me that all the world must be barren, like what I see of it. In the country we forget the town, and in town we despise the country. "Beyond Hyde Park," says Sir Fopling Flutter, "all is a desert." All that part of the map that we do not see before us is blank. The world in our conceit of it is not much bigger than a nutshell. It is not one prospect expanded into another, county joined to county, kingdom to kingdom, land to seas, making an image voluminous and vast;— the mind can form no larger idea of space than the eye can take in at a single glance. The rest is a name written in a map, a calculation of arithmetic. For instance, what is the true signification of that immense mass of territory and population known by the name of China to us? An inch of pasteboard on a wooden globe, of no more account than a China orange! Things near us are seen of the size of life: things at a distance are diminished to the size of the understanding. We measure the universe by ourselves, and even comprehend the texture of our own being only piecemeal. In this way, however, we remember an infinity of things and places. The mind is like a mechanical instrument that plays a great variety of tunes, but it must play them in succession. One idea recalls another, but it at the same time excludes all others. In trying to renew old recollections, we cannot as it were unfold the whole web of our existence; we must pick out the single threads. So in coming to a place where we have formerly lived, and with which we have intimate associations, every one must have found that the feeling grows more vivid the nearer we approach the spot, from the mere anticipation of the actual impression: we remember circumstances, feelings, persons, faces, names that we had not thought of for years; but for the time all the rest of the world is

forgotten !—To return to the question I have quitted
above :—

I have no objection to go to see ruins, aqueducts,
pictures, in company with a friend or a party, but
rather the contrary, for the former reason reversed.
They are intelligible matters, and will bear talking
about. The sentiment here is not tacit, but com-
municable and overt. Salisbury Plain is barren of
criticism, but Stonehenge will bear a discussion anti-
quarian, picturesque, and philosophical. In setting
out on a party of pleasure, the first consideration
always is where we shall go to : in taking a solitary
ramble, the question is what we shall meet with by the
way. " The mind is its own place ; " nor are we
anxious to arrive at the end of our journey. I can
myself do the honours indifferently well to works of
art and curiosity. I once took a party to Oxford
with no mean *éclat*—showed them that seat of the
Muses at a distance,

"With glistering spires and pinnacles adorn'd—"

descanted on the learned air that breathes from the
grassy quadrangles and stone walls of halls and col-
leges—was at home in the Bodleian ; and at Blenheim
quite superseded the powdered cicerone that attended
us, and that pointed in vain with his wand to commonplace beauties in matchless pictures. As another
exception to the above reasoning, I should not feel
confident in venturing on a journey in a foreign
country without a companion. I should want at
intervals to hear the sound of my own language.
There is an involuntary antipathy in the mind of an
Englishman to foreign manners and notions that re-
quires the assistance of social sympathy to carry it
off. As the distance from home increases, this relief,
which was at first a luxury, becomes a passion and an
appetite. A person would almost feel stifled to find

himself in the deserts of Arabia without friends and countrymen : there must be allowed to be something in the view of Athens or old Rome that claims the utterance of speech ; and I own that the Pyramids are too mighty for any single contemplation. In such situations, so opposite to all one's ordinary train of ideas, one seems a species by one's-self, a limb torn off from society, unless one can meet with instant fellowship and support. Yet I did not feel this want or craving very pressing once, when I first set my foot on the laughing shores of France. Calais was peopled with novelty and delight. The confused, busy murmur of the place was like oil and wine poured into my ears ; nor did the mariners' hymn, which was sung from the top of an old crazy vessel in the harbour, as the sun went down, send an alien sound into my soul. I only breathed the air of general humanity. I walked over " the vine-covered hills and gay regions of France," erect and satisfied ; for the image of man was not cast down and chained to the foot of arbitrary thrones : I was at no loss for language, for that of all the great schools of painting was open to me. The whole is vanished like a shade. Pictures, heroes, glory, freedom, all are fled : nothing remains but the Bourbons and the French people !—There is undoubtedly a sensation in travelling into foreign parts that is to be had nowhere else ; but it is more pleasing at the time than lasting. It is too remote from our habitual associations to be a common topic of discourse or reference, and, like a dream or another state of existence, does not piece into our daily modes of life. It is an animated but a momentary hallucination. It demands an effort to exchange our actual for our ideal identity ; and to feel the pulse of our old transports revive very keenly, we must " jump " all our present comforts and connections. Our romantic and itinerant character is not to be domesticated. Dr. Johnson remarked how little foreign travel added to the facilities of conversation in those who had been abroad. In fact, the time we have spent there is both delightful, and in one sense instructive ; but it appears to be cut out of our substantial, downright existence, and never to join kindly on to it. We are not the same, but another, and perhaps more enviable individual, all the time we are out of our own country. We are lost to ourselves, as well as our friends. So the poet somewhat quaintly sings :

" Out of my country and myself I go."

Those who wish to forget painful thoughts, do well to absent themselves for a while from the ties and objects that recall them ; but we can be said only to fulfil our destiny in the place that gave us birth. I should on this account like well enough to spend the whole of my life in travelling abroad, if I could anywhere borrow another life to spend afterwards at home !

JOHN ADDINGTON SYMONDS

1840–1893

Personal Style

I

A SURVEY of language, however superficial, makes it evident that when we speak of style, we have to take into account those qualities of national character which are embodied in national speech. If two men could be born of precisely the same physical, mental, and moral nature, at precisely the same moment of history, and under precisely the same social conditions ; and if these men learned different languages in the cradle, and used those languages in after life, they would be unable to deliver exactly the same message to the world through literature. The dominant qualities of each mother-tongue would impose definite limitations on their power of expressing thoughts, however similar or identical those thoughts might be.

We cannot conceive two men born with the same physical, mental, and moral nature, at the same moment, under precisely the same conditions, and using the same language. They would be identical ; and everything they uttered would be clothed with exactly the same words. The absurdity of this conception brings home to us the second aspect of style. Style is not merely a sign of those national qualities which are generic to established languages, and which constitute the so-called genius of a race. It is also the sign of personal qualities, specific to individuals, which constitute the genius of a man. Whatever a man utters from his heart and head is the index of his character. The more remarkable a person is, the more strongly he is differentiated from the average of human beings, the more salient will be the characteristic notes of his expression. But even the commonest people have, each of them, a specific style. The marks of difference become microscopical as we descend from Dante or Shakespeare to the drudges of the clerk's desk in one of our great cities. Yet these marks exist, and are no less significant of individuality than the variations between leaf and leaf upon the lime-trees of an avenue.

It may be asked whether the manner of expression peculiar to any person is a complete index to his character—whether, in other words, there is " an art to find the mind's construction " in the style. Not altogether and exhaustively. Not all the actions and the utterances of an individual betray the secret of his personality. You may live with men and women through years, by day, by night, yet you will never know the whole about them. No human being knows the whole about himself.

The deliberate attitude adopted by a literary writer implies circumspection ; invites suppression, reservation, selection ; is compatible with affectation, dissimulation, hypocrisy. So much cannot be claimed for critical analysis as that we should pretend to reproduce a man's soul after close examination of his work. What we may assert with confidence is that the qualities of style are intimately connected with the qualities and limitations of the writer, and teach us much about him. He wrote thus and thus, because he was this or this. In the exercise of style it is impossible for any one to transcend his inborn and acquired faculties of ideation, imagination, sense-

perception, verbal expression—just as it is impossible
in the exercise of strength for an athlete to transcend
the limits of his physical structure, powers of inner-
vation, dexterity, and courage. The work of art
produced by a writer is therefore of necessity com-
plexioned and determined by the inborn and acquired
faculties of the individual. This is what we mean by
the hackneyed epigram : " Le style c'est l'homme."

II

Certain broad distinctions of moral and emotional
temperament may undoubtedly be detected in literary
style. A tendency toward exaggeration, toward self-
revelation, toward emphasis upon the one side ; a
tendency to reserve, to diminished tone in colouring,
to parsimony of rhetorical resource upon the other ;
these indicate expansiveness or reticence in the writer.
Victor Hugo differs by the breadth of the whole
heavens from Leopardi. One man is ironical by
nature, another sentimental. Sterne and Heine have
a common gift of humour ; but the quality of humour
in each case is conditioned by sympathetic or by
caustic undercurrents of emotion. Sincerity and affectation, gaiety and melancholy, piety and scepticism,
austerity and sensuality penetrate style so subtly and
unmistakably that a candid person cannot pose as the
mere slave of convention, a boon companion cannot
pass muster for an anchorite, the founder of a religious
sect cannot play the part of an agnostic. In dramatic
work the artist creates characters alien from his own
personality, and exhibits people widely different from
himself acting and talking as they ought to do. This
he achieves by sympathy and intuition. Yet all
except the very greatest fail to render adequately
what they have not felt and been. In playwrights
of the second order, like our Fletcher, or of the third
order, like our Byron, the individual who writes the

tragedy and shapes the characters is always apparent under every mask he chooses to assume. And even the style of the greatest, their manner of presenting the varieties of human nature, betrays individual peculiarities. Æschylus sees men and women differently from Sophocles, Corneille from Racine, Shakespeare from Goethe.

In like manner the broad distinctions of mental temperament may be traced in style. The abstract thinker differs from the concrete thinker in his choice of terms ; the analytical from the synthetic ; the ratiocinative from the intuitive ; the logical from the imaginative ; the scientific from the poetical. One man thinks in images, another in formal propositions. One is diffuse, and gets his thought out by reiterated statement. Another makes epigrams, and finds some difficulty in expanding their sense or throwing light upon them by illustrations. One arrives at conclusions by the way of argument. Another clothes assertion with the tropes and metaphors of rhetoric.

The same is true of physical and æsthetical qualities. They are felt inevitably in style. The sedentary student does not use the same figures of speech as come naturally to the muscular and active lover of field sports. According as the sense for colour, or for sound, or for light, or for form shall preponderate in a writer's constitution, his language will abound in references to the world, viewed under conditions of colour, sound, light, or form. He will insensibly dwell upon those aspects of things which stimulate his sensibility and haunt his memory. Thus, too, predilections for sea or mountains, for city life or rural occupations, for flowers, precious stones, scents, birds, animals, insects, different kinds of food, torrid or temperate climates, leave their mark on literary style.

Acquired faculties and habits find their expression in style no less than inborn qualities. Education, based upon humanism or scientific studies ; contact with powerful personalities at an impressible period of youth ; enthusiasm aroused for this or that great masterpiece of literature ; social environment ; high or low birth ; professional training for the bar, the church, medicine, or commerce ; life in the army, at sea, upon a farm, and so forth, tinge the mind and give a more or less perceptible colour to language.

The use of words itself yields, upon analysis, valuable results illustrative of the various temperaments of authors. A man's vocabulary marks him out as of this sort or that sort—his preference for certain syntactical forms, for short sentences or for periods, for direct or inverted propositions, for plain or figurative statement, for brief or amplified illustrations. Some compose sentences, but do not build paragraphs —like Emerson ; some write chapters, but cannot construct a book. Nor is punctuation to be disregarded, inasmuch as stops enable us to measure a writer's sense of time-values, and the importance he attaches to several degrees of rest and pause.

III

It is impossible to do more than indicate some of the leading points which illustrate the meaning of the saying that style is the man ; any one can test them and apply them for himself. We not only feel that Walter Scott *did not* write like Thackeray, but we also know that he *could not* write like Thackeray, and vice versa. This impossibility of one man producing work in exactly the same manner as another makes all deliberate attempts at imitation assume the form of parody or caricature. The sacrifice of individuality involved in scrupulous addiction to one great master of Latin prose, Cicero, condemned the best stylists of the Renaissance—men like Muretus—to lifeless and eventually worthless production. Meanwhile the exact psychology is wanting which would render our intuitions regarding the indissoluble link between style and personal character irrefutable.

Literary style is more a matter of sentiment, emotion, involuntary habits of feeling and observing, constitutional sympathy with the world and men, tendencies of curiosity and liking, than of the pure intellect. The style of scientific works, affording little scope for the exercise of these psychological elements, throws less light upon their authors' temperament than does the style of poems, novels, essays, books of travel, descriptive criticism. In the former case all that need be aimed at is lucid exposition of fact and vigorous reasoning. In the latter the fact to be stated, the truth to be arrived at, being of a more complex nature, involves a process akin to that of the figurative arts. The stylist has here to produce the desired effect by suggestions of infinite subtlety, and to present impressions made upon his sensibility.

Autobiographies, epistolary correspondence, notes of table-talk, are of the highest value in determining the correlation between a writer's self and his style. We not only derive a mass of information about Goethe's life from Eckermann, but we also discover from those conversations in how true a sense the style of Goethe's works grew out of his temperament and experience. Gibbon and Rousseau, Alfieri and Goldoni, Samuel Johnson in his *Life* by Boswell, John Stuart Mill in his autobiographical essay, Petrarch in his *Secretum* and fragment of personal confessions, have placed similar keys within our reach for unlocking the secret of their several manners.

The rare cases in which men of genius have excelled in more than one branch of art are no less instructive. Michelangelo the sonnet-writer helps us to understand Michelangelo the sculptor. Rossetti the painter throws light on Rossetti the poet ; William Blake the lyrist upon William Blake the draughtsman. We find

on comparing the double series of work offered by
such eminent and exceptionally gifted individuals,
that their styles in literature and plastic art possess
common qualities, which mark the men and issue
from their personalities. Michelangelo in the sonnets
is as abstract, as ideal, as form-loving, as indifferent
to the charm of brilliant colour, as neglectful of ex-
ternal nature as Michelangelo in his statues and the
frescoes of the Sistine Chapel. Rossetti's pictures,
with their wealth of colour, their elaborate execution,
their sharp incisive vision, their deep imaginative
mysticism and powerful perfume of intellectual sen-
suousness, present a close analogue to his ballads,
sonnets, and descriptive poems. With these and
similar instances in our mind, we are prepared to hear
that Victor Hugo designed pictures in the style of
Gustave Doré ; nor would it surprise us to discover
that Gustave Doré had left odes or fiction in the manner of Victor Hugo.

The problems suggested by style as a sign and index
of personality may be approached from many points
of view. I have not aimed at exhaustiveness even
of suggestion in my treatment of the topic ; and while
saying much which will appear perhaps trivial and
obvious, have omitted some of the subtler and more
interesting aspects of the matter. A systematic
criticism of personal style would require a volume,
and would demand physiological and psychological
knowledge which is rarely found in combination with
an extensive study of literatures and arts.

R. L. STEVENSON

Random Memories

I

THROUGH what little channels, by what hints and pre-monitions, the consciousness of the man's art dawns first upon the child, it should be not only interesting but instructive to inquire. A matter of curiosity to-day, it will become the ground of science to-morrow. From the mind of childhood there is more history and more philosophy to be fished up than from all the printed volumes in a library. The child is conscious of an interest, not in literature but in life. A taste for the precise, the adroit, or the comely in the use of words, comes late ; but long before that he has en-joyed in books a delightful dress rehearsal of experi-ence. He is first conscious of this material—I had almost said this practical—pre-occupation ; it does not follow that it really came the first. I have some old fogged negatives in my collection that would seem to imply a prior stage. " The Lord is gone up with a shout, and God with the sound of a trumpet "—memorial version, I know not where to find the text —rings still in my ear from my first childhood, and perhaps with something of my nurse's accent. There was possibly some sort of image written in my mind by these loud words, but I believe the words them-selves were what I cherished. I had about the same time, and under the same influence—that of my dear

nurse—a favourite author : it is possible the reader
has not heard of him—the Rev. Robert Murray
M'Cheyne. My nurse and I admired his name ex-
ceedingly, so that I must have been taught the love
of beautiful sounds before I was breeched ; and I
remember two specimens of his muse until this day :—

> " Behind the hills of Naphtali
>   The sun went slowly down,
> Leaving on mountain, tower, and tree,
>   A tinge of golden brown."

There is imagery here, and I set it on one side. The
other—it is but a verse—not only contains no image,
but is quite unintelligible even to my comparatively
instructed mind, and I know not even how to spell
the outlandish vocable that charmed me in my childhood—

> " Jehovah Tschidkenu is nothing to her " ;—

I may say, without flippancy, that he was nothing to
me either, since I had no ray of a guess of what he was
about ; yet the verse, from then to now, a longer
interval than the life of a generation, has continued
to haunt me.

I have said that I should set a passage distinguished
by obvious and pleasing imagery, however faint ; for
the child thinks much in images, words are very live
to him, phrases that imply a picture eloquent beyond
their value. Rummaging in the dusty pigeon-holes
of memory, I came once upon a graphic version of the
famous Psalm, " The Lord is my shepherd " ; and
from the places employed in its illustration, which
are all in the immediate neighbourhood of a house
then occupied by my father, I am able to date it
before the seventh year of my age, although it was
probably earlier in fact. The " pastures green " were
represented by a certain suburban stubble-field,

where I had once walked with my nurse, under an autumnal sunset, on the banks of the Water of Leith : the place is long ago built up ; no pastures now, no stubble-fields ; only a maze of little streets and smoking chimneys and shrill children. Here, in the fleecy person of a sheep, I seemed to myself to follow something unseen, unrealized, and yet benignant ; and close by the sheep in which I was incarnated—as if for greater security—rustled the skirts of my nurse. "Death's dark vale" was a certain archway in the Warriston Cemetery : a formidable yet beloved spot, for children love to be afraid,—in measure as they love all experience of vitality. Here I beheld myself some paces ahead (seeing myself, I mean, from behind) utterly alone in that uncanny passage ; on the one side of me a rude, knobby, shepherd's staff, such as cheers the heart of the cockney tourist, on the other a rod like a billiard cue, appeared to accompany my progress ; the staff sturdily upright, the billiard cue inclined confidentially, like one whispering, towards my ear. I was aware—I will never tell you how—that the presence of these articles afforded me encouragement. The third and last of my pictures illustrated the words :—

> "My table Thou hast furnished
> In presence of my foes :
> My head Thou dost with oil anoint,
> And my cup overflows : "

and this was perhaps the most interesting of the series. I saw myself seated in a kind of open stone summer-house at table ; over my shoulder a hairy, bearded, and robed presence anointed me from an authentic shoe-horn ; the summer-house was part of the green court of a ruin, and from the far side of the court black and white imps discharged against me ineffectual arrows. The picture appears arbitrary, but I can trace every detail to its source, as Mr.

Brock analyzed the dream of Alan Armadale. The summer-house and court were muddled together out of Billings' *Antiquities of Scotland ;* the imps conveyed from Bagster's *Pilgrim's Progress ;* the bearded and robed figure from any one of the thousand Bible pictures ; and the shoe-horn was plagiarized from an old illustrated Bible, where it figured in the hand of Samuel anointing Saul, and had been pointed out to me as a jest by my father. It was shown me for a jest, remark ; but the serious spirit of infancy adopted it in earnest. Children are all classics ; a bottle would have seemed an intermediary too trivial—that divine refreshment of whose meaning I had no guess ; and I seized on the idea of that mystic shoe-horn with delight, even as, a little later, I should have written flagon, chalice, hanaper, beaker, or any word that might have appealed to me at the moment as least contaminate with mean associations. In this string of pictures I believe the gist of the psalm to have consisted ; I believe it had no more to say to me ; and the result was consolatory. I would go to sleep dwelling with restfulness upon these images ; they passed before me, besides, to an appropriate music ; for I had already singled out from that rude psalm the one lovely verse which dwells in the minds of all, not growing old, not disgraced by its association with long Sunday tasks, a scarce conscious joy in childhood, in age a companion thought :—

> " In pastures green Thou leadest me,
>   The quiet waters by."

The remainder of my childish recollections are all of the matter of what was read to me, and not of any manner in the words. If these pleased me it was unconsciously ; I listened for news of the great vacant world upon whose edge I stood ; I listened for delightful plots that I might re-enact in play, and romantic scenes and circumstances that I might call up before me, with closed eyes, when I was tired of Scotland, and home, and that weary prison of the sick-chamber in which I lay so long in durance. *Robinson Crusoe ;* some of the books of that cheerful, ingenious, romantic soul, Mayne Reid ; and a work rather gruesome and bloody for a child, but very picturesque, called *Paul Blake ;* these are the three strongest impressions I remember : *The Swiss Family Robinson* came next, *longo intervallo.* At these I played, conjured up their scenes, and delighted to hear them rehearsed unto seventy times seven. I am not sure but what *Paul Blake* came after I could read. It seems connected with a visit to the country, and an experience unforgettable. The day had been warm ; H—— and I had played together charmingly all day in a sandy wilderness across the road ; then came the evening with a great flash of colour and a heavenly sweetness in the air. Somehow my playmate had vanished, or is out of the story, as the sages say, but I was sent into the village on an errand ; and, taking a book of fairy tales, went down alone through a fir-wood, reading as I walked. How often since then has it befallen me to be happy even so ; but that was the first time: the shock of that pleasure I have never since forgot, and if my mind serves me to the last, I never shall, for it was then that I knew I loved reading.

II

To pass from hearing literature to reading it is to take a great and dangerous step. With not a few, I think a large proportion of their pleasure then comes to an end ; " the malady of not marking " overtakes them ; they read thenceforward by the eye alone and hear never again the chime of fair words or the march of the stately period. *Non ragionam* of these. But to all the step is dangerous ; it involves coming of age ; it is even a kind of second weaning. In the past all was at the choice of others ; they chose, they digested, they read aloud for us and sang to their own tune the books of childhood. In the future we are to approach the silent, inexpressive type alone, like pioneers ; and the choice of what we are to read is in our own hands thenceforward. For instance, in the passages already adduced, I detect and applaud the ear of my old nurse ; they were of her choice, and she imposed them on my infancy, reading the works of others as a poet would scarce dare to read his own ; gloating on the rhythm, dwelling with delight on assonances and alliterations. I know very well my mother must have been all the while trying to educate my taste upon more secular authors ; but the vigour and the continual opportunities of my nurse triumphed, and after a long search, I can find in these earliest volumes of my autobiography no mention of anything but nursery rhymes, the Bible, and Mr. M'Cheyne.

I suppose all children agree in looking back with delight on their school Readers. We might not now find so much pathos in " Bingen on the Rhine," " A Soldier of the Legion lay dying in Algiers," or in "The Soldier's Funeral," in the declamation of which I was held to have surpassed myself. " Robert's voice," said the master on this memorable occasion, " is not strong, but impressive : " an opinion which I was fool enough to carry home to my father ; who roasted me for years in consequence. I am sure one should not be so deliciously tickled by the humorous pieces :—

" What, crusty ? cries Will in a taking,
   Who would not be crusty with half a year's baking ? "

Non ragionam, Let us not talk.   (Quotation from Dante.)

I think this quip would leave us cold. The " Isles of Greece " seem rather tawdry too ; but on the " Address to the Ocean," or on " The Dying Gladiator," " time has writ no wrinkle."

> "'Tis the morn, but dim and dark,
> Whither flies the silent lark ? "—

does the reader recall the moment when his eye first fell upon these lines in the Fourth Reader ; and " surprised with joy, impatient as the wind," he plunged into the sequel ? And there was another piece, this time in prose, which none can have forgotten ; many like me must have searched Dickens with zeal to find it again, and in its proper context, and have perhaps been conscious of some inconsiderable measure of disappointment, that it was only Tom Pinch who drove, in such a pomp of poetry, to London.

But in the Reader we are still under guides. What a boy turns out for himself, as he rummages the bookshelves, is the real test and pleasure. My father's library was a spot of some austerity ; the proceedings of learned societies, some Latin divinity, cyclopædias, physical science, and, above all, optics, held the chief place upon the shelves, and it was only in holes and corners that anything really legible existed as by accident. The *Parent's Assistant, Rob Roy, Waverley,* and *Guy Mannering,* the *Voyages of Captain Woods Rogers,* Fuller's and Bunyan's *Holy Wars, The Reflections of Robinson Crusoe, The Female Bluebeard,* G. Sand's *Mare au Diable*—(how came it in that grave assembly !), Ainsworth's *Tower of London,* and four old volumes of *Punch*—these were the chief exceptions. In these latter, which made for years the chief of my diet, I very early fell in love (almost as soon as I could spell) with the Snob Papers. I knew them almost by heart, particularly the visit to the Pontos ; and I remember my surprise when I found, long afterwards, that they were famous, and signed with a famous name ; to me, as I read and admired them, they were the works of Mr. Punch. Time and again I tried to read *Rob Roy*, with whom of course I was acquainted from the *Tales of a Grandfather ;* time and again the early part, with Rashleigh and (think of it !) the adorable Diana, choked me off ; and I shall never forget the pleasure and surprise with which, lying on the floor one summer evening, I struck of a sudden into the first scene with Andrew Fairservice. " The worthy Dr. Lightfoot "—" mistrysted with a bogle "—" a wheen green trash "—" Jenny, lass, I think I ha'e her " ; from that day to this the phrases have been unforgotten. I read on, I need scarce say ; I came to Glasgow, I bided tryst on Glasgow Bridge, I met Rob Roy and the Bailie in the Tolbooth, all with transporting pleasure ; and then the clouds gathered once more about my path ; and I dozed and skipped until I stumbled half-asleep into the clachan of Aberfoyle, and the voices of Iverach and Galbraith recalled me to myself. With that scene and the defeat of Captain Thornton the book concluded ; Helen and her sons shocked even the little schoolboy of nine or ten with their unreality ; I read no more, or I did not grasp what I was reading ; and years elapsed before I consciously met Diana and her father among the hills, or saw Rashleigh dying in the chair. When I think of that novel and that evening, I am impatient with all others ; they seem but shadows and impostors ; they cannot satisfy the appetite which this awakened ; and I dare be known to think it the best of Sir Walter's by nearly as much as Sir Walter is the best of novelists. Perhaps Mr. Lang is right, and our first friends in the land of fiction are always the most real. And yet I had read before this *Guy Mannering*, and some of *Waverley*, with no such delighted sense of truth and humour, and I read immediately after the greater part of the Waverley Novels, and was never moved again in the same way or to the same degree. One circumstance is suspicious : my critical estimate of the Waverley Novels has scarce changed at all since I was ten. *Rob Roy, Guy Mannering,* and *Redgauntlet* first ; then, a little lower, *The Fortunes of Nigel ;* then, after a huge gulf, *Ivanhoe* and *Anne of Geierstein :* the rest nowhere ; such was the verdict of the boy. Since then *The Antiquary, St. Ronan's Well, Kenilworth,* and *The Heart of Midlothian* have gone up in the scale ; perhaps *Ivanhoe* and *Anne of Geierstein* have gone a trifle down ; Diana Vernon has been added to my admirations in that enchanted world of *Rob Roy ;* I think more of the letters in *Redgauntlet,* and Peter Peebles, that dreadful piece of realism, I can now read about with equanimity, interest, and I had almost said pleasure, while to the childish critic he often caused unmixed distress. But the rest is the same ; I could not finish *The Pirate* when I was a child, I have never finished it yet ; *Peveril of the Peak* dropped half-way through from my schoolboy hands, and though I have since waded to an end in a kind of wager with myself, the exercise was quite without enjoyment. There is something disquieting in these considerations. I still think the visit to Ponto's the best part of the *Book of Snobs :* does that mean that I was right when I was a child, or does it mean that I have never grown since then, that the child is not the man's father, but the man ? and that I came into the world with all my faculties complete, and have only learned sinsyne to be more tolerant of boredom ? . . .

The Ideal House

Two things are necessary in any neighbourhood where we propose to spend a life : a desert and some living water.

There are many parts of the earth's face which offer the necessary combination of a certain wildness with a kindly variety. A great prospect is desirable, but the want may be otherwise supplied ; even greatness can be found on the small scale ; for the mind and the eye measure differently. Bold rocks near hand are more inspiriting than distant Alps, and the thick fern upon a Surrey heath makes a fine forest for the imagination, and the dotted yew trees noble mountains. A Scottish moor with birches and firs grouped here and there upon a knoll, or one of those rocky seaside deserts of Provence overgrown with rosemary and thyme and smoking with aroma, are places where the mind is never weary. Forests, being more enclosed, are not at first sight so attractive, but they exercise a spell ; they must, however, be diversified with either heath or rock, and are hardly to be considered perfect without conifers. Even sand-hills, with their intricate plan, and their gulls and rabbits, will stand well for the necessary desert.

The house must be within hail of either a little river or the sea. A great river is more fit for poetry than to adorn a neighbourhood ; its sweep of waters increases the scale of the scenery and the distance of one notable object from another ; and a lively burn gives us, in the space of a few yards, a greater variety of promontory and islet, of cascade, shallow goil, and boiling pool, with answerable changes both of song and colour, than a navigable stream in many hundred miles. The fish, too, make a more considerable feature of the brookside, and the trout plumping in the shadow takes the ear. A stream should, besides, be narrow enough to cross, or the burn hard by a bridge, or we are at once shut out of Eden. The quantity of water need be of no concern, for the mind sets the scale, and can enjoy a Niagara Fall of thirty inches. Let us approve the singer of

> "Shallow rivers, by whose falls
> Melodious birds sing madrigals."

If the sea is to be our ornamental water, choose an open seaboard with a heavy beat of surf ; one much broken in outline, with small havens and dwarf headlands ; if possible a few islets ; and as a first necessity, rocks reaching out into deep water. Such a rock on a calm day is a better station than the top of Teneriffe or Chimborazo. In short, both for the desert and the water, the conjunction of many near and bold details is bold scenery for the imagination and keeps the mind alive.

Given these two prime luxuries, the nature of the country where we are to live is, I had almost said, indifferent ; after that inside the garden, we can construct a country of our own. Several old trees, a considerable variety of level, several well-grown hedges to divide our garden into provinces, a good extent of old well-set turf, and thickets of shrubs and evergreens to be cut into and cleared at the new owner's pleasure, are the qualities to be sought for in your chosen land. Nothing is more delightful than a succession of small lawns, opening one out of the other through tall hedges ; these have all the charm of the old bowling-green repeated, do not require the labour of many trimmers, and afford a series of changes. You must have much lawn against the early summer, so as to have a great field of daisies, the year's morning frost ; as you must have a wood of lilacs, to enjoy to the full the period of their blossoming. Hawthorn is another of the Spring's ingredients ; but it is even best to have a rough public lane at one side of your enclosure which, at the right season, shall become an avenue of bloom and odour. The old flowers are the best and should grow carelessly in corners. Indeed, the ideal fortune is to find an old garden, once very richly cared for, since sunk into neglect, and to tend, not repair, that neglect ; it will thus have a smack of nature and wildness which skilful dispositions cannot overtake. The gardener should be an idler, and have a gross partiality to the kitchen plots : an eager or toilful gardener misbecomes the garden landscape ; a tasteful gardener will be ever meddling, will keep the borders raw, and take the bloom off nature. Close adjoining, if you are in the south, an olive-yard, if in the north, a swarded apple-orchard reaching to the stream, completes your miniature domain ; but this is perhaps best entered through a door in the high fruit-wall ; so that you close the door behind you on your sunny plots, your hedges and evergreen jungle, when you go down to watch the apples falling in the pool. It is a golden maxim to cultivate the garden for the nose, and the eyes will take care of themselves. Nor must the ear be forgotten : without birds a garden is a prison-yard. There is a garden near Marseilles on a steep hill-side, walking by which, upon a sunny morning, your ear will suddenly be ravished with a burst of small and very cheerful singing : some score of cages being set out there to sun their occupants. This is a heavenly surprise to any passer-by ; but the price paid, to keep so many ardent and winged creatures from their liberty, will make the luxury too dear for any thoughtful pleasure-lover. There is only one sort of bird that I can tolerate caged, though even then I think it hard, and that is what is called in France the Bec-d'Argent. I once had two of these pigmies in captivity ; and in the quiet, bare house upon a silent street where I was then living, their song, which was not much louder than a bee's, but airily musical, kept me in a perpetual good humour. I put the cage upon my table when I worked, carried it with me when I went for meals, and kept it by my head at night : the first thing in the morning, these *maestrini* would pipe up. But these, even if you can pardon their imprisonment, are for the house. In the garden the wild birds must plant a colony, a chorus of the lesser warblers that should be almost deafening, a blackbird in the lilacs, a nightingale down the lane, so that you must stroll to hear it, and yet a little farther, tree-tops populous with rooks.

Your house should not command much outlook ; it should be set deep and green, though upon rising ground, or, if possible, crowning a knoll, for the sake of drainage. Yet it must be open to the east, or you will miss the sunrise ; sunset occurring so much later, you can go up a few steps and look the other way. A house of more than two stories is a mere barrack ; indeed the ideal is of one story, raised upon cellars. If the rooms are large, the house may be small : a single room, lofty, spacious, and lightsome, is more palatial than a castleful of cabinets and cupboards. Yet size in a house, and some extent and intricacy of corridor, is certainly delightful to the flesh. The reception room should be, if possible, a place of many recesses, which are " petty retiring places for conference " ; but it must have one long wall with a divan : for a day spent upon a divan, among a world of cushions, is as full of diversion as to travel. The eating-room, in the French mode, should be *ad hoc :* unfurnished, but with a buffet, the table, necessary chairs, one or two of Canaletto's etchings, and a tile fire-place for the winter. In neither of these public places should there be anything beyond a shelf or two of books ; but the passages may be one library from end to end, and the stair, if there be one, lined with volumes in old leather, very brightly carpeted, and leading half-way up, and by way of landing, to a windowed recess with a fire-place ; this window, almost alone in the house, should command a handsome prospect. Husband and wife must each possess a studio ; on the woman's sactuary I hesitate to dwell and turn to the man's. The walls are shelved waist-high for books, and the top thus forms a continuous table running round the wall. Above are prints, a large map of the neighbourhood, a Corot and a Claude or two. The room is very spacious, and the five tables and two chairs are but as islands. One table is for actual work, one close by for references in use ; one, very large, for MSS. or proofs that wait their turn ; one kept clear for an occasion ; and the fifth is the map table, groaning under a collection of large-scale maps and charts. Of all books these are the least wearisome to read and the richest in matter ; the course of roads and rivers, the contour lines and the forests in the maps—the reefs, soundings, anchors, sailing marks and little pilot-pictures in the charts— and, in both, the bead-roll of names, make them of all printed matter the most fit to stimulate and satisfy the fancy. The chair in which you write is very low and easy, and backed into a corner ; at one elbow the fire twinkles ; close at the other, if you are a little inhumane, your cage of silver-bills are twittering into song.

Joined along by a passage, you may reach the great, sunny, glass-roofed, and tiled gymnasium, at the far end of which, lined with bright marble, is your plunge and swimming bath, fitted with a capacious boiler.

The whole loft of the house from end to end makes one undivided chamber ; here are set forth tables on which to model imaginary or actual countries in putty or plaster, with tools and hardy pigments ; a carpenter's bench ; and a spared corner for photography, while at the far end a space is kept clear for playing soldiers. Two boxes contain the two armies of some five hundred horse and foot ; two others the ammunition of each side, and a fifth the foot-rules and the three colours of chalk, with which you lay down, or, after a day's play, refresh the outlines of the country ; red or white for the two kinds of road (according as they are suitable or not for the passage of ordnance), and blue for the course of the obstructing rivers. Here I foresee that you may pass much happy time ; against a good adversary a game may well continue for a month ; for with armies so considerable three moves will occupy an hour. It will be found to set an excellent edge on this diversion if one of the players shall, every day or so, write a report of the operations in the character of army correspondent.

I have left to the last the little room for winter evenings. This should be furnished in warm positive colours, and sofas and floor thick with rich furs. The hearth, where you burn wood of aromatic quality on silver dogs, tiled round about with Bible pictures ; the seats deep and easy ; a single Titian in a gold frame ; a white bust or so upon a bracket ; a rack for the journals of the week ; a table for the books of the year ; and close in a corner the three shelves full of eternal books that never weary : Shakespeare, Molière, Montaigne, Lamb, Sterne, De Musset's comedies (the one volume open at *Carmosine* and the other at *Fantasio*) ; the *Arabian Nights*, and kindred stories, in Weber's solemn volumes ; Borrow's *Bible in Spain*, the *Pilgrim's Progress*, *Guy Mannering* and *Rob Roy*, *Monte Cristo* and the *Vicomte de Bragelonne*, immortal Boswell sole among biographers, Chaucer, Herrick, and the *State Trials*.

The bedrooms are large, airy, with almost no furniture, floors of varnished wood, and at the bed-head, in case of insomnia, one shelf of books of a particular and dippable order, such as *Pepys*, the *Paston Letters*, Burt's *Letters from the Highlands*, or the *Newgate Calendar*. . . .

MRS. MEYNELL

The Illusion of Historic Time

HE who has survived his childhood intelligently must become conscious of something more than a change in his sense of the present and in his apprehension of the future. He must be aware of no less a thing than the destruction of the past. Its events and empires stand where they did, and the mere relation of time is as it was. But that which has fallen together, has fallen in, has fallen close, and lies in a little heap, is the past itself—time—the fact of antiquity.

He has grown into a smaller world as he has grown older. There are no more extremities. Recorded time has no more terrors. The unit of measure which he holds in his hand has become in his eyes a thing of paltry length. The discovery draws in the annals of mankind. He had thought them to be wide.

For a man has nothing whereby to order and place the floods, the states, the conquests, and the temples of the past, except only the measure which he holds. Call that measure a space of ten years. His first ten years had given him the illusion of a most august scale and measure. It was then that he conceived Antiquity. But now ! Is it to a decade of ten such little years as these now in his hand—ten of his mature years—that men give the dignity of a century ? They call it an age ; but what if life shows now so small that the word age has lost its gravity ?

In fact, when a child begins to know that there is a

past, he has a most noble rod to measure it by—he has his own ten years.   He attributes an overwhelming majesty to all recorded time.   He confers distance. He, and he alone, bestows mystery.   Remoteness is his.   He creates more than mortal centuries.   He sends armies fighting into the extremities of the past. He assigns the Parthenon to a hill of ages, and the temples of Upper Egypt to sidereal time.

If there were no child, there would be nothing old. He, having conceived old time, communicates a remembrance at least of the mystery to the mind of the man.   The man perceives at last all the illusion, but he cannot forget what was his conviction when he was a child.   He had once a persuasion of Antiquity. And this is not for nothing.   The enormous undeception that comes upon him still leaves spaces in his mind.

But the undeception is rude work.   The man receives successive shocks.   It is as though one strained level eyes towards the horizon, and then were bidden to shorten his sight and to close his search within a poor half acre before his face.   Now it is that he suddenly perceives the hitherto remote, remote youth of his own parents to have been something familiarly near, so measured by his new standard ; again it is the coming of Attila that is displaced.   Those ten last years of his have corrected the world.   There needs no other rod than that ten years' rod to chastise all the imaginations of the spirit of man.   It makes history skip.

To have lived through any appreciable part of any century is to hold thenceforth a mere century cheap enough.   But, it may be said, the mystery of change remains.   Nay, it does not.   Change that trudges through our own world—our contemporary world— is not very mysterious.   We perceive its peace ; it is a jog-trot.   Even so, we now consider, jolted the changes of the past, with the same hurry.

The man, therefore, who has intelligently ceased to be a child scans through a shortened avenue the reaches of the past. He marvels that he was so deceived. For it was a very deception. If the Argonauts, for instance, had been children, it would have been well enough for the child to measure their remoteness and their acts with his own magnificent measure. But they were only men and demi-gods. Thus they belong to him as he is now—a man ; and not to him as he was once—a child. It was quite wrong to lay the child's enormous ten years' rule along the path from our time to theirs ; that path must be skipped by the nimble yard in the man's present possession. Decidedly the Argonauts are no subject for the boy.

What, then ? Is the record of the race nothing but a bundle of such little times ? Nay, it seems that childhood, which created the illusion of ages, does actually prove it true. Childhood is itself Antiquity— to every man his only Antiquity. The recollection of childhood cannot make Abraham old again in the mind of a man of thirty-five ; but the beginning of every life is older than Abraham. *There* is the abyss of time. Let a man turn to his own childhood—no farther—if he would renew his sense of remoteness, and of the mystery of change.

For in childhood change does not go at that mere hasty amble ; it rushes ; but it has enormous space for its flight. The child has an apprehension not only of things far off, but of things far apart ; an illusive apprehension when he is learning " ancient " history—a real apprehension when he is conning his own immeasurable infancy. If there is no historical Antiquity worth speaking of, this is the renewed and unnumbered Antiquity for all mankind.

And it is of this—merely of this—that " ancient " history seems to partake. Rome was founded when we began Roman history, and that is why it seems long ago. Suppose the man of thirty-five heard, at that present age, for the first time of Romulus. Why, Romulus would be nowhere. But he built his wall, as a matter of fact, when every one was seven years old. It is by good fortune that " ancient " history is taught in the only ancient days. So, for a time, the world is magical.

Modern history does well enough for learning later. But by learning something of antiquity in the first ten years, the child enlarges the sense of time for all mankind. For even after the great illusion is over and history is re-measured, and all fancy and flight caught back and chastised, the enlarged sense remains enlarged. The man remains capable of great spaces of time. He will not find them in Egypt, it is true, but he finds them within, he contains them, he is aware of them. History has fallen together, but childhood surrounds and encompasses history, stretches beyond and passes on the road to eternity.

He has not passed in vain through the long ten years, the ten years that are the treasury of perceptions—the first. The great disillusion shall never shorten those years, nor set nearer together the days that made them. " Far apart," I have said, and that " far apart " is wonderful. The past of childhood is not single, is not motionless, nor fixed in one point ; it has summits a world away one from the other. Year from year differs as the antiquity of Mexico from the antiquity of Chaldea. And the man of thirty-five knows for ever afterwards what is flight, even though he finds no great historic distances to prove his wings by.

There is a long and mysterious moment in long and mysterious childhood, which is the extremest distance known to any human fancy. Many other moments, many other hours, are long in the first ten years. Hours of weariness are long—not with a mysterious length, but with a mere length of protraction, so that the things called minutes and half-hours by the elderly may be something else to their apparent contemporaries, the children. The ancient moment is not merely one of these—it is a space not of long, but of immeasurable, time. It is the moment of going to sleep. The man knows that borderland, and has a contempt for it : he has long ceased to find antiquity there. It has become a common enough margin of dreams to him ; and he does not attend to its phantasies. He knows that he has a frolic spirit in his head which has its way at those hours, but he is not interested in it. It is the inexperienced child who passes with simplicity through the marginal country ; and the thing he meets there is principally the yet further conception of illimitable time.

His nurse's lullaby is translated into the mysteries of time. She sings absolutely immemorial words. It matters little what they may mean to waking ears ; to the ears of a child going to sleep they tell of the beginning of the world. He has fallen asleep to the sound of them all his life ; and " all his life " means more than older speech can well express.

Ancient custom is formed in a single spacious year. A child is beset with long traditions. And his infancy is so old, so old, that the mere adding of years in the life to follow will not seem to throw it farther back— it is already so far. That is, it looks as remote to the memory of a man of thirty as to that of a man of seventy. What are a mere forty years of added later life in the contemplation of such a distance ? Pshaw !

July

ONE has the leisure of July for perceiving all the differences of the green of leaves. It is no longer a difference in degrees of maturity, for all the trees have darkened to their final tone, and stand in their differences of character and not of mere date. Almost all the green is grave, not sad and not dull. It has a darkened and a daily colour, in majestic but not obvious harmony with dark grey skies, and might look, to inconstant eyes, as prosaic after spring as eleven o'clock looks after the dawn.

Gravity is the word—not solemnity as towards evening, nor menace as at night. The daylight trees of July are signs of common beauty, common freshness, and a mystery familiar and abiding as night and day. In childhood we all have a more exalted sense of dawn and summer sunrise than we ever fully retain or quite recover ; and also a far higher sensibility for April and April evenings—a heartache for them, which in riper years is gradually and irretrievably consoled.

But, on the other hand, childhood has so quickly learned to find daily things tedious, and familiar things importunate, that it has no great delight in the mere middle of the day, and feels weariness of the summer that has ceased to change visibly. The poetry of mere day and of late summer becomes perceptible to mature eyes that have long ceased to be sated, have taken leave of weariness, and cannot now find anything in nature too familiar ; eyes which have, indeed, lost sight of the further awe of midsummer daybreak, and no longer see so much of the past in April twilight as they saw when they had no past ; but which look freshly at the dailiness of green summer, of early afternoon, of every sky of any form that comes to pass, and of the darkened elms.

Not unbeloved is this serious tree, the elm, with its leaf sitting close, unthrilled. Its stature gives it a dark gold head when it looks alone to a late sun. But if one could go by all the woods, across all the old forests that are now meadowlands set with trees, and could walk a county gathering trees of a single kind in the mind, as one walks a garden collecting flowers of a single kind in the hand, would not the harvest be a harvest of poplars ? A veritable passion for poplars is a most intelligible passion. The eyes do gather them, far and near, on a whole day's journey. Not one is unperceived, even though great timber should be passed, and hillsides dense and deep with trees. The fancy makes a poplar day of it. Immediately the country looks alive with signals ; for the poplars everywhere reply to the glance. The woods may be all various, but the poplars are separate.

All their many kinds (and aspens, their kin, must be counted with them) shake themselves perpetually free of the motionless forest. It is easy to gather them. Glances sent into the far distance pay them a flash of recognition of their gentle flashes ; and as you journey you are suddenly aware of them close by. Light and the breezes are as quick as the eyes of a poplar-lover to find the willing tree that dances to be seen.

No lurking for them, no reluctance. One could never make for oneself an oak day so well. The oaks would wait to be found, and many would be missed from the gathering. But the poplars are alert enough for a traveller by express ; they have an alarum aloft, and do not sleep. From within some little grove of other trees a single poplar makes a slight sign ; or a long row of poplars suddenly sweep the wind. They are salient everywhere, and full of replies. They are as fresh as streams.

It is difficult to realize a drought where there are many poplars. And yet their green is not rich ; the coolest have a colour much mingled with a cloud-grey. It does but need fresh and simple eyes to recognize their unfaded life. When the other trees grow dark and keep still, the poplar and the aspen do not darken —or hardly—and the deepest summer will not find a day in which they do not keep awake. No waters are so vigilant, even where a lake is bare to the wind.

When Keats said of his Dian that she fastened up her hair " with fingers cool as aspen leaves," he knew the coolest thing in the world. It is a coolness of colour, as well as of a leaf which the breeze takes on both sides—the greenish and the greyish. The poplar green has no glows, no gold ; it is an austere colour, as little rich as the colour of willows, and less silvery than theirs. The sun can hardly gild it ; but he can shine between. Poplars and aspens let the sun through with the wind. You may have the sky sprinkled through them in high midsummer, when all the woods are close.

Sending your fancy poplar-gathering, then, you ensnare wild trees, beating with life. No fisher's net ever took such glancing fishes, nor did the net of a constellation's shape ever enclose more vibrating Pleiades.

MAURICE HEWLETT

The Maypole and the Column

In days of more single purpose than these, young men and maidens, in the first flush of summer, set up a maypole on the green ; but before they joined hands and danced round about it they had done honour to what it stood for by draping it with swags of flowers and green-stuff, hanging it with streamers of divers colours, and sticking it with as many gilt hearts as there were hearts among them of votive inclination. So they transfigured the thing signified, and turned a shaven tree-trunk from a very crude emblem into a thing of happy fantasy. That will serve me for a figure of how the poet deals with his little idea, or great one ; and in his more sober mood it is open to the essayist so to deal with his, supposing he have one. He must hang his pole, or concept, not with rhyme but with wise or witty talk. He must turn it about and about, not to set the ornaments jingling, or little bells ringing ; rather that you may see its shapeliness enhanced, its proportions emphasized, and in all the shifting lights and shadows of its ornamentation discern it still for the notion that it is. That at least is my own notion of what the essayist should do, though I am aware that very distinguished practitioners have not agreed with me and do not agree at this hour. The modern essayist, for reasons which I shall try to expound, has been driven from the maypole to the column.

Certainly, the parent of the Essay draped no maypoles with speech. Montaigne was a sedentary philosopher, of the order of the post-prandials; a wine-and-walnuts man. One thing would open out into another, and one seem better than the other, at the time of hearing. " Je n'enseigne point; je raconte," he tells you of himself; and it is true. To listen to him is a liberal education; yet you can hardly think of Montaigne footing it on the green. Bacon's line, again, was the aphoristic. He shreds off his maypole rather than clothes it: but he has one set up. He can give his argument as witty a turn as the Frenchman when he pleases—" There is no man doth a wrong for the wrong's sake, but thereby to purchase himself profit, or pleasure, or honour, or the like. Therefore why should I be angry with a man for loving himself better than me?" That is the turn his thoughts take upon Revenge, and a fair sample of his way with an abstract idea—shredding off it all the time, getting down to the pith. But he can be very obscure: " A single life doth well with Churchmen; for charity will hardly water the ground where it must first fill a pool." That is proleptic reasoning. We are to caper about the pole before the ornaments are on.

But since his time the Maypole has gone out of use. The modern essayist has had a column reared for him instead, which he is required, not to drape, but to fill. That kind of column is no symbol of the earth's fertility, but too often the grave of it. It has been, however, the opportunity of the babbler, the prater, the prattler, and the agreeable rattle: all's one to the Column so that it be filled. You may write on something, or nothing; you may grind axes on your column, or roll logs on it. But you must fill it. To be too long for it is nothing. There is the Procrustean sword. To be too short——Minotaur will howl for more.

Hazlitt is the typical journalist-essayist. He could fill a column with any man born, yet not with pure gain to literature. He makes an ungracious figure in history, unsocial and anti-social too, with his blundering, uncouth loves, his undignified quarrels, and insatiable hatreds. His spleen engulfed him, and I have often wondered what our Wiltshire shepherds made of him, lowering like a storm about the coombes of Winterslow. None of the " pastoral melancholy " of that grassy solitude shows in his writing, whose zest is that of hunger rather than wholesome appetite. Indeed, I don't think he was a tolerable essayist. He was too eager to destroy, and the very moral of his own John Bull who would sooner, any day, give up an estate than a bugbear. How many people he hated, and how much ! Whole nations at once—such as the French. He hated Southey and Gifford, and for their sakes the *Quarterly*, Pitt and Castlereagh, Byron and Coleridge. He was a fierce lover, too, but not comfortable in his loves. Sometimes he knew both passions for the same person. Burke, for instance : *Odi et amo*, he said of him. He had that bad symptom of the violent lover, that he could only honour his love at another's expense. So Racine and Walter Scott must be trampled under foot before Shakespeare can be duly esteemed. There is consequently a sense of strain in reading Hazlitt which his fine raptures (and no writer soared more rapturously) can only overcome on select occasions. His account of Cavanagh the fives player is one, his essay on John Buncle another. For once, for twice, he was single-minded, and forgot to hurt anybody.

He learned length from the Reviews, which encouraged the essay to be a treatise, and have many a tedious page. Illustrations press upon him and cannot be refused. He has that trick of saying the same thing several times in slightly different ways which was common to all the essayists of his time, doomed to fill their columns. Procter, Leigh Hunt, and Lamb all did that—Lamb less tiresomely than any ; for Lamb enhanced the image, or shifted it into happier view, with every addition. But Hazlitt left it where it was, or hid it.

Lamb was essayist first, and journalist with what remained over. A column was set up : he made it a maypole. No craftsman has draped his idea, or capered about it as Lamb did. He transfigures whatever he touches ; more, he transmutes it. His seventeenth-century jargon, which you may find tiresome, is part of the fun. It is, so to speak, joco-serious with him. He is generally better without it, as in " Blakesmoor " or " Barbara S——," or " Dream-Children " ; yet of all Elia the most beautiful thing to me is one which has Burton and Sir Thomas Browne all over it, " A Quakers' Meeting." There you have exactly what I mean by my overworked figure of the Maypole. A theme set up, and hung with loving art ; then round about it a measure trodden, sedately for the most part, but with involuntary skips aside as the whim takes him. Lamb could not spare a joke even at a funeral ; but this is sheer beauty, a serene and lovely close :—

" The very garments of a Quaker seem incapable of receiving a soil ; and cleanliness in them to be something more than the absence of its contrary. Every Quakeress is a lily ; and when they come up in bands to their Whitsun conferences, whitening the easterly streets of the metropolis, from all parts of the United Kingdom, they show like troops of the Shining Ones."

That is to do more than dance about a maypole. It is to dance before the Lord.

All the pieces which follow* were written for and published in daily newspaper or weekly or monthly review : the *Times* and *Manchester Guardian, Nation*

---

* This was originally written as a Preface to a volume of essays.

and *Outlook, Nineteenth Century and After, London Mercury, Cornhill.* Well or ill, they were intended to deck their column as if it had been a maypole. Rightly or wrongly, they were to be literature as well as journalism. Journalism loves the particular, but literature must hold fast to the general. Journalism accepts the ephemeral, gives you its daily screed in exchange for its daily bread ; but literature has its eye on posterity, expresses the spirit of fact rather than the body of it ; and its servants, if not exacting a monument more perdurable than brass, wish that they may get, and try to deserve it. Genius does what it must, and need not concern us here. Shakespeare wrote *Hamlet* for hire, and Walter Scott *The Bride of Lammermoor,* that he might add field to field by Tweedside. They had their monument without a thought thrown that way. And Keats, who said that his name was writ in water ? Did he not know that it was writ in ink, which grows blacker with age ? But let the smaller man do consciously and with premeditation what his betters did by the Grace of God. No man needs be the worse journalist for taking immense pains to be something beside.

It is hard work. " I never have a holiday. On Monday towards noon I lift up my head, and breathe for about an hour ; after that the wicket shuts again and I am in my prison cell for seven days." So said Sainte-Beuve ; and Matthew Arnold comments upon the saying, " The *causeries* were at this price." Hard work——but the only way to serve your two masters, turn your column into a maypole and pace out your dedicatory dance.

Montaigne

WE owe the Press many things, not all of them gladly ; but for one thing at least we may be its thankful debtors, and that is that it has allowed, if not engaged, the Essay to survive. From the days of Addison the essayist has been journalist too, and that which cost Montaigne a lifetime has thereafter been compassed within the year, if not to its advantage, then to its perennity. That is an accident of public economy, however, which is beside the matter, for both Montaigne and Bacon were very capable of journalism for all their leisurely habit. One was deeply versed in affairs, the other kept a wary eye for them and knew, as we put it, the time of day with the best. But politics was not Montaigne's business, who if he had been living to-day would be one of our best " middle " practitioners, a writer deliberately desultory, occasional ; " fluctuating and various," as he said ; a man not always, and never purposely, didactic, but, as he went on, not far from the vein of Polonius ; a full man, however, bursting with anecdote, and one of a singularly detached, dry, not to say frosty, judgment. I could name the weekly which he would adorn, and those which would have none of him. And the daily also. There is but one. I think he would be welcomed there.

The Essay may be *décousu* if the essayist pleases, and as Montaigne certainly did—that is, if himself is so. It is better thus, for the general, than that it should be crabbed, though personally I like close writing. It may, indeed, be both crabbed and desultory ; and that was Montaigne's way ; for however much he might meander he had a serried mind and massed himself upon his points as they turned up. That was by no means in any orderly sequence, as he proves abundantly by thrusting his tenderest reminiscences of his father into his Essay *De l' Yvrongnerie*, with which the worthy man had nothing at all to do. He slips into them by exclaiming, " C'est merveille des contes que j'ay ouy faire à mon père de la chasteté de son siècle," and breaks them off abruptly with, " Revenons à nos bouteilles." That is so de-

sultory as to be casual ; yet the simplicity of hand-
ling rids it of offence. He adored his father. The
occasion of his writing Essays may account for the
form which they took. He began by making extracts
from the Classics into a commonplace book. Thereafter, when a subject occurred to him, he looked
through his notes, picked his quotations, and there,
practically, you were. He picked too many, and used
them all. Some of his early essays merely strung
them together like beads. But he set the fashion
which did not forsake us till the other day (and then
for a very good reason) and became a quarry for his
disciples, as Burton of the *Anatomy* also became.
Men went to Montaigne, not to follow out his vagaries
but to stimulate their own. As he grew more into the
work he was doing he improved vastly upon his first
attempts. He kept closer to life, dealt less in general
ideas. His citations then had point, by ceasing to be
the only point. He is at his highest in his Third Book,
as in "Sur des Vers de Virgile," and "Du Repentir,"
and very nearly as good in the twelfth essay of the
Second Book : "Apologie de Raimond de Sebonde."
In each of those three he has a subject close to his
heart—Love, Himself, Mankind. There, having something better to do, he makes the classics fetch and
carry for him. Nobody who desires to know to what
point detachment can be carried without ceasing to
be human can afford to neglect the "Apologie." It is
the best alterative conceivable for what ills an excessive use of *Gulliver's Travels* may have induced in the
reader. " J'ay veu en mon temps cent artisans, cent
laboureurs, plus sages et plus heureux que des Rec-
teurs de l'Université." And again, "La peste de
l'homme c'est l'opinion de sçavoir." And once more,
" Notre bien-estre, ce n'est que la privation d'estre
mal. Voylà pourquoy la secte de philosophie qui a
le plus faict valoir la volupté encore a-elle rangée à la
seule indolence." The last is a paradox which I don't

admit, except as a masterly reduction of facts to an
absurdity. As you read you can see the frosty old
eyelids glimmering over it.

With those and certain other exceptions, I don't
pretend to idolatrous admiration of Montaigne. I
will play with anybody at anything up and down the
world, but must know what game it is we are playing. Montaigne does not. There never was a man
who cared less for sum-m-ject and om-m-ject. Though
he prefers to handle general notions, he takes them
by the handful at a time ; and I don't believe you
will find a core of idea in an essay of his. Sometimes
he will intend for one and never reach it. There is an
essay of good length in the Second Book called " Cous-
tume de l'Isle de Cea," in which there is not a word
either of the island or the custom, whatever it was.
He had not reached them, I suppose, by the time he
was tired. One in the Third Book, "Des Coches,"
opens with a discussion of the habit of blessing the
sneezer—a pretty oblique attack. But one does not
go to Montaigne to find a theme stated, or disquisi-
tion festooned about a peg. He is one to be opened
at hazard ; a good man for the *sortes*. You will find
wisdom on every page : " Le prix de l'âme ne consiste
pas à aller haut, mais ordonnément. Sa grandeur ne
s'exerce par de la grandeur, c'est en la médiocrité ; "
many a sharp sentence : " Nos folies ne me font pas
rire ; c'est nos sapiences " ; a pungency, a salt ; but
you will seldom be touched either to laughter or tears ;
and for a kindly old man, as he surely was, he is
curiously without charm. He had friends—he tells
us so ; but they were few, and in general he held men
at arm's length. " La froideur de ma conversation
m'a desrobé avec raison la bienvaillance de plusieurs."
How many friends has he made since his death ?
Think of him beside Burton, Sir Thomas Browne,
Charles Lamb. If the whole of his book had been as
the last half of it we might have had a different feeling

towards him. If his heart had gone in, ours might have gone out. His writing mellows as it goes on, as no doubt he did himself. Whether it tells us anything is another matter.

> " With this key
> Shakespeare unlocked his heart . . ."

that is, with the sonnet. Can that be said of Montaigne and the Essay ? If the essayist is not personal he is nought, and may as well class himself pamphleteer at once. Personal they have been, one and all, importing their egos into any argument whatsoever, allowing no other staple, considering no appeals. Except lyric poetry, I suppose there is no such fun in the world, given the knack, as essay-writing. You write of what you know best and love best. "Son plus laborieux et principal estude c'est s'estudier soy," Montaigne reported of his own wit. That is by no means to say that he publishes all his discoveries. Other things besides interest go into the study. Vanity goes in ; prejudice is never out. Humility may be under the table, and modesty have her back to the wall. When you read Montaigne upon *le Repentir* you may think he has told you everything, so much has he the air of having discharged his bosom. Analyse the essay and you will find that he has indeed been frank about his tower, chamber, library, and *basse-cour*, but singularly discreet about himself and his own plenishings. A word or two of his habits— eating, drinking, sleeping : nothing else, and nothing that matters. After studying the subject for forty years, that is not all he had learned. It is what he has thought fit to tell, and I don't think that either modesty or humility held his hand.

For that apparent candour and real secretiveness, I conclude, and not because he was perfectly calm about the St. Bartholomew and the like of that, Michelet could not find a good word to say for him. Certainly, if a man is writing the History of France he may be pardoned for losing patience with a man or with mankind. Man as he ought not to be was good enough for Montaigne, whose historical researches went no further than the fall of the Roman Empire, and could not have discovered him much about the French one even if he had been concerned about it. No doubt also that he took more interest in Man than in men. He was ever a solitary. He mentions the Wars of Religion rarely, and mostly as a bore. He reports that he has seen men burnt for religion's sake—" ces pauvres gens "—and has remarked their wild devotions in the midst of the fire. By such exercises, he deems, they kept the faith, or rather they gave it new direction ; which, he goes on, says much for their piety, little for their constancy. His is woundily right, as usual, but it is a hard saying. There are not many more references to passing events: the execution of Mary Stuart is one, and no reprobation for it. He calls François II., her first husband, the greatest king in Christendom, which is a compliment probably to the realm rather than to the little monarch. As for his own beliefs, he professed himself a Catholic, and purposed to live and die in that persuasion—as in fact he did. For all that appears he was what we call a deist. The *Paternoster* was enough prayer for him ; but there is as little about the Saviour in the *Essais* as there is in *Lycidas*, nothing of the Madonna, nothing of the hierarchies except a good story of an old woman who was found with two tapers alight before the altar of St. Michael, one for him and one for the dragon. I think Montaigne burnt his candles in duplicate too. He was, and professed to be, the man of common sense, the average concupiscent male who had contrived to temper appetite by maintaining an accurate view of the consequences of indulgence. He positively declined to regret anything he had done. " Si j'avois à revivre, je revivrais comme j'ay vescu."

That is the saying of a very sincere or very foolish man. Myself, I believe him.

I have been led away from the *Essais* to consider the Essayist, a vain exercise if I am right in thinking that he purposely spun himself out of sight in them. No matter for that : he has done his work, done it so well that from his day to our own the form has persisted without any material change. If one had to define the Essay it would be as the written, after-dinner monologue of a well-read, well-satisfied man of, at least, five-and-forty. Years don't matter : the spirit of years matters very much. You must be mature enough to pontificate and wise enough to do it tactfully. You must not be long, you should not be difficult ; you may be discursive, but not abrupt. You may eschew eloquence and outrageous fun ; you should subserve the chuckle. You may bedew the eyes, not drown them. You may not take sides, nor improve the occasion. Your teaching must be by the way. " Je n'enseigne point," Montaigne says, " je raconte." You will be allusive, of course—all full men are so ; and you will quote freely, often inaccurately. Anecdote should be your salt, but I don't think quotation should be your pepper.

It was Montaigne's undoubtedly, and, like his anecdotes, almost entirely of one people and language. It was very well for his auditory of the moment which, with him, spoke Latin at least as well as French—he himself spoke it better. But that implacable people, the Romans, have receded far from us. Neither Troy nor Rome stands where it did. Our essayists have since discovered other nations. First it was Israel, and you had Abishai and Aholibah, Hophni and Phineas walking familiarly in the page ; next it was Shakespeare ; and now we have more Keats than we really need. But certainly we are more temperate, or more ignorant, than our fathers ; and at least we are short. So had I better be.

ARTHUR CLUTTON-BROCK

The Defects of English Prose

I CANNOT read Mr. Pearsall Smith's anthology of English Prose without thinking of the anthology I would make myself and wondering all the while why his differs from mine. Why, among writers of the past, does he omit Shaftesbury and give but one passage from Johnson, when he gives so many from Sir Thomas Browne ? Why is there not more of Gibbon's wit, and why not his great passage upon the funeral and character of Julian the Apostate ? Why so many short, laboured, and not profound sentences from Carlyle, followed by but one extract from Newman ? Why the Gioconda passage from Pater, which has the defect that it is false ? Why no Dickens at all, and no William Morris, and no W. H. Hudson ? The answer is that Mr. Pearsall Smith lays his own emphasis in this anthology and I should lay another. For him our prose is greatest when it is nearest to poetry ; it is overshadowed by our poetry and almost its poor relation. A Frenchman reading his anthology might say : " All this is magnificent, but it is hardly prose. This is the literature of a people that can sing and preach, but cannot converse. I listen with amazement to all these prophets, but I should not care to talk with them ; for, to tell the truth, they are not civilized. They do not seem to be men like myself, only abler ; they are chiefs or elders at a tribal gathering, practising the eloquence of barbarians."

Yet there is another side to English prose which Mr. Pearsall Smith almost ignores : perhaps because he is making an anthology and that other side cannot easily be exhibited in extracts. Prose of its very nature is longer than verse, and the virtues peculiar to it manifest themselves gradually. If the cardinal virtue of poetry is love, the cardinal virtue of prose is justice ; and, whereas love makes you act and speak on the spur of the moment, justice needs inquiry, patience, and a control even of the noblest passions. But English Prose, as Mr. Pearsall Smith presents it, is at the mercy of its passions and just only by accident. By justice here I do not mean justice only to particular people or ideas, but a habit of justice in all the processes of thought, a style tranquillized and a form moulded by that habit. The master of prose is not cold, but he will not let any word or image inflame him with a heat irrelevant to his purpose. Unhasting, unresting, he pursues it, subduing all the riches of his mind to it, rejecting all beauties that are not germane to it ; making his own beauty out of the very accomplishment of it, out of the whole work and its proportions, so that you must read to the end before you know that it is beautiful. But he has his reward, for he is trusted and convinces, as those who are at the mercy of their own eloquence do not ; and he gives a pleasure all the greater for being hardly noticed. In the best prose, whether narrative or argument, we are so led on as we read, that we do not stop to applaud the writer : nor do we stop to question him. But we stop, whether to applaud or to question, at a sentence such as this, which Mr. Pearsall Smith gives us from Carlyle—

" Brave Sea captain, Norse Sea-king Columbus, my hero, royalest Sea-king of all! it is no friendly environment this of thine, in the waste deep waters : round thee mutinous discouraged souls, behind thee disgrace and ruin, before thee the unpenetrated veil of Night."

If a writer continues long in this style, he wearies us like a man talking at the top of his voice ; and if he does not continue, the passage distracts us with its incongruity, like a sudden shouting. Carlyle here, and often, yields to a habit of excitement as if he had a right to be indulged in it. He is like a man who will make speeches at the dinner-table to show the force of his convictions. These are the manners of egotism, and egotism is the worst of all faults in prose.

For prose is the achievement of civilization, of people who have learned to discuss without blows or invective, who know that truth is hard to find and worth finding, who do not begin by accusing an opponent of wickedness, but elicit reason and patience by displaying them. You cannot say in poetry what the best prose says, or accomplish what the best prose accomplishes. Civilization may not surpass a primitive society in heights of rapture or heroism, but it is, if it be civilization, better for everyday life, kinder, more rational, more sustained in effort ; and this kindness and reason and sustained effort are expressed and encouraged in the masterpieces of prose. The French understood this long ago, because they prize civilization and enjoy it. Pascal, writing his *Provincial Letters* in 1656 upon a subject obscured by mediæval subtleties and distorted by party passions, is already just, polite, and lucid ; he does not even affect the magnificent disdain of Gibbon, but is a civilized man talking to other civilized men, and therefore all the more deadly in debate. But it is fallacies that he would kill, not those who maintain them. He knows that the art of controversy is, not to begin with invective, but to state your case in such a way that those who like invective will supply it themselves against your adversary.

So we read Milton's controversy for its accidents, splendid as they are, but Pascal's still for the controversy itself. Though he is not clothed in shining armour, he fights for the children of light in all ages, with no pretence of being an angel or a dervish, but quietly appealing to the everlasting reason from whence comes his help. In this book of Mr. Pearsall Smith's, with its array of great names and great passages, we notice how his moderns seem to archaize when they would soar, as if they must pretend to be of the giant race before the flood so as to believe in their own greatness. Emerson says :—

"Our friendships hurry to short and poor conclusions, because we have made them a texture of wine and dreams, instead of the tough fibre of the human heart."

Ruskin, even in *Præterita*, writes thus of his first sight of the Alps :—

"Infinitely beyond all that we had ever thought or dreamed—the seen walls of lost Eden could not have been more beautiful to us ; not more awful round Heaven, the walls of sacred Death."

Pater begins a paragraph :—

"I have remarked how in the process of our brain-building, as the house of thought in which we live gets itself together like some airy bird's nest of floating thistle-down and chance straws, compact at last, little accidents have their consequence."

Stevenson, in a letter, and talking of familiar things, says :—

"Methought you asked me—frankly, was I happy ? Happy (said I) ; I was happy only once ; that was at Hyères ; it came to an end from a variety of reasons, decline of health, change of place, increase of money,

age with his stealing steps ; since then, as before then,
I know not what it means."

It is always finely, but not naturally, said.

Each writer seems to have a model not quite suited
to the matter or the occasion, and makes us think of
this model when we should be thinking only of what
he has to say.   But the prose which interests us most,
and persuades us unconsciously to go on reading it,
seems to be made by the matter and the occasion ;
it is like talk between intimates, and the writer draws
us into intimacy by his manner of address, which
assumes that we do not wish to be tricked or dazzled,
that, if he has anything worth saying, we shall listen
to it for its own sake.

There is less of this prose in our literature than we
could wish, but more than we should gather from Mr.
Pearsall Smith's anthology.   It began to be written
about the time of the Restoration by Cowley, Halifax,
and Dryden among others.   Mr. Pearsall Smith gives
one short passage from Cowley, one from Halifax, and
none from Dryden—perhaps he thinks that the best
of Dryden's prose is in his verse.   But the first easy
master of it is Shaftesbury, especially in his *Letter
concerning Enthusiasm.*   Here the case is all the more
remarkable because he is talking of religion and saying
things both novel and profound about it.   His plea
is for good humour in controversy, and he gives an
example of it in his own letter.   He begins lightly
enough, and then, with a humane and natural art,
leads us into seriousness :—

"This, my Lord, is the security against superstition : To remember that there is nothing in God but
what is God-like ; and that He is either not at all
or truly and perfectly good.   But when we are afraid
to use our reason freely, even on that very question,
'Whether He really be, or not ' ; we then actually

presume Him bad, and flatly contradict that pretended character of goodness and greatness, whilst we discover this mistrust of His temper, and fear His anger and resentment in the case of this freedom of inquiry."

But though this is just and even now fresh, we cannot deny that it lacks the music and images of Jeremy Taylor or Milton ; and they are absent from the prose of Johnson and all the eighteenth century. For that reason the Romantics despised even its virtues ; for them, again, prose became the poor relation of poetry, and must wear its cast-off clothes ; or else they wrote like orators addressing a crowd with repetitions and loud emphasis, abrupt transitions and noisy images. Hazlitt is more eloquent than scrupulous ; he never seems to be alone with you as you read him, but rather speaking to catch votes, even though it be for the best writers or painters ; and Macaulay, ignored by Mr. Pearsall Smith, is worse. His prose has all the defects of a nation political rather than social, he is incapable of meditation or even of converse, but lectures always ; while Burke writes of the Sublime and Beautiful like an orator.

So, but for a few shy, never enough honoured writers, there is one whole province of the English mind left out of our prose, for we are capable of meditation and intimate talk ; we are more civilized than our manners or our style. Mr. W. H. Hudson, for instance, seems always to be meditating or remembering ; writing for him is a means of saying what he would never say aloud. He makes his dearest friend of the reader, and confides in him with speech that has the beauty of a wild animal's eyes. And Mark Rutherford, with a different kind of matter but the same shyness and melancholy faith, arouses a like confidence in us. These writers seldom say much in a single sentence or even paragraph, but they have a cumulative power that cannot be proved by quotation, a wandering music that blows where it lists, because they never force their inspiration or tell you what they have not got to say. Their peculiar quality is justice ; they describe without a laboured eagerness or momentum, and without vivid words, just what they have seen and felt. They do not exploit their loves or their hatreds, and it is wonderful that you should remember so well what is said with so little emphasis or apparent skill of words. Yet it is remembered, like a thought that does not need saying ; it sinks deep into the mind, beyond language, like an actual experience, and, if you read their books with care, you are changed as if by an event.

But such writers are likely to remain few, for they are little encouraged. We are not yet a public of readers civilized enough to demand the highest virtues of prose ; we prefer " clamorous sublimities " and phrases that ask to be noticed ; we must be urged through a book by the crack of the writer's whip. Yet still one dreams of a prose that has never yet been written in English, though the language is made for it and there are minds not incapable of it, a prose dealing with the greatest things quietly and justly as men deal with them in their secret meditations, seeming perhaps to wander, but always advancing in an unbroken sequence of thought, with a controlled ardour of discovery and the natural beauties of a religious mind. Johnson might have written it, if he had had a stronger sense of beauty and more faith in the flights of reason ; Newman if he had been a greater master of words and less afraid of his own questioning ; Henry James if he had exercised his subtlety on larger things. But the best of our prose writers, living or dead, are not civilized enough, or too much in love with something else, or not enough in love with anything, to write the prose we dream of. The English Plato is still to be.

MARY E. COLERIDGE

Gifts

THERE are gifts that are no gifts, just as there are books that are no books. A donation is not a gift.

A portrait painted—a teapot presented—by subscription, is not a gift. The giving is divided among too many. The true gift is from one to one. Furthermore, tea, sugar, and flannel petticoats are not gifts. If I bestow these conveniences on one old woman, she may regard them in that aspect ; but if I bestow them on eleven others at the same time, she looks upon them as her right. By giving more I have given less. The dole is no more like the gift than charity is like love. A £50 cheque on the occasion of a marriage between Blank and Blank is not a gift ; it is a transfer of property.

And why is it *de rigueur* that if somebody I like goes into partnership with somebody she likes, I must give her an enormous silver buttonhook when she has six already ? The pleasure I confer on her by doing so is not worth the value of the penny stamp which she must, equally *de rigueur*, waste on informing me that she is pleased. It is not within the bounds of possibility that a human being can appreciate more than—say fifty presents at a time, when she has to write notes for them all. The line should be drawn at fifty—for large and generous natures at seventy ; and all friends who have not sent in their buttonhooks before a certain date should be requested to distribute them over the coming years instead. As a lily in winter, so is the unexpected gift. But the gift that arrives by tens and tens of tens is a nightmare and an oppression.

Again, the periodical gift is never refreshing ; it is too much of the nature of tribute. A present on Midsummer Day would be worth two at Christmas.

> " The free gift only cometh of the free."

The articles of furniture—lamps, matchboxes, footstools, and so on—duly exchanged between members of the same family, at certain seasons, are not gifts. They are a kind of tax levied by duty on liking, and duty claims the credit of them. Liking responds with what is called gratitude—a doubtful virtue at best, impossible between true friends—too near obsequiousness in the poor, too hollow for sincerity in the rich. There is no element of surprise about these presents. The spirit of giving is killed by regularity. How can I care—except in a material way—for what is part of my annual income ? The heart is not interested. I get these things because my name is down on a piece of paper, not because some one is possessed with an impatient desire to please or to share pleasure.

Rarely, among the many things that are passed from hand to hand, is one a gift ; and the giver is not so common as he was. System has attacked and ruined him even in the nursery. Santa Claus no longer comes down the chimney on Christmas Eve as he (or she) did when the child was never sure what might be in his stocking. As soon as he can write at all— or sooner—the child writes a list of " Christmas wishes," and these are conscientiously fulfilled by his father and mother, who know a great deal more than his grandfather and grandmother knew, only they do not know—unless he tells them—what it is that he wants. A feeling of depressed amazement stole over me one day when I heard a little girl enumerating the items on her list :—

> A Writing-desk.
> A Muff.
> A Prayer-book.
> A Whole Family of Giraffes.

What sort of mother could that have been who was not aware that her daughter wanted A Whole Family of Giraffes unless she saw it in black and white ? And as for the Writing-desks and Muffs and Prayer-books, the child ought to have had them anyhow. We should never have thought such things were presents at all when we were young ; the bare necessities of life!

No. A gift—to be a gift—must not be asked for. Dante laid down this rule, with many others, which lead one to reflect that it must have been difficult to give him a present. The request is payment; he who receives in this case buys, though he who gives cannot be accused of selling. The poet also decrees that a gift which is not so valuable to the recipient as it would be to the giver is no true gift. Romantic generosity would have been spared many a pang, had she considered this precept. *The Falcon* would not have been cooked for dinner ; the life of *The Kentucky Cardinal* might have been saved. People who have pearls are curiously fond of stringing them together and offering them to pigs. It makes the pig unhappy in the end.

There is a third saying of Dante, which is a counsel of perfection ; the face of the gift should resemble the face of him to whom the gift is given. If this be so, only those who understand each other's appearance should venture to give. My friend, who has an expression like a beautiful sermon, must not present me with a volume of Lightfoot when French novels are written all over my speaking countenance. Neither must I inflict on her the works of " Gyp."

It is a complicated business altogether. Three minutes of serious thinking make it impossible for any one to give any one anything. Yet the deed is done every year boldly and openly, and few are sensible that they have undertaken a more delicate transaction than the robbery of a Bank in broad daylight.

When Rosalind, at a moment's notice, gave Orlando the chain from her neck, the action was perfect on her side and on his. Any man a little lower than Shakespeare would have made Orlando show it and talk about it in the forest ; he would not have let it pass without a single further allusion. Celia remembers, she teases Rosalind ; but the two lovers will never speak of it again. There was no merit in Rosalind ; she gave because she could not help herself. How could Orlando thank her except in silence ? Like another young gentleman in the same circumstances, he had been little happy could he have said how much.

There is in some natures a high intolerance of the airy fetters cast round the heart by the constant memory of beneficence. They give freely, but freely they do not receive. They must send something by return of post, like the two friends in *Elizabeth and her German Garden*, who regularly transmitted to each other the same candlestick and the same notebook turn about, as each anniversary chimed the hour on their clocks—whereby they saved an incalculable amount of time, money, and emotion. One sweet lady goes so far as to say that all presents should be of perishable character—a basket of fruit, a bunch of flowers—that they may be at once forgotten.

Yet, if the truth were known, it might be found that the smaller, the more insignificant the gift, the longer it is remembered. There may be many motives for keeping the Golden Rose ; there can be only one for keeping a rose-leaf. Thus was it said by a man of old time who knew what a woman liked and gave her a distaff : " Great grace goes with a little gift, and all the offerings of friends are precious."

On Paper Matches

IT is the costliest entertainment that can be devised, this burning of paper. The pearl that Cleopatra threw into her wine when she pledged Anthony was nothing to it. Burn a piece of blank paper alone—a white sheet ; upon that surface of snow the man alive who is nearest Milton might have written his intent. You are consuming the stuff that immortality is made of. But to burn a piece of paper with words upon it —this is to be like Helen, to fire another *Troy*. What ! For this hand, eye, and human brain worked in a three-fold harmony ! For this the marvellous creature, ink, was made—that blackness holding the colours of the rainbow! For this the pen was sharpened from the wing of a bird—from the torn veins of Mother Earth ! For this the dress that covered a princess, the rags that kept a beggar from the cold, were ground in mills as though they had been corn—simply that you might be, not warmer, but for a second brighter ! I never destroy a letter—as I never put out a candle— without regret, or savage joy. Either way I have killed something.

A friend told me once that, unless she burnt a letter the instant after reading, the task was more difficult every day. It grew into the Past—it became history. If she burnt it at once, she was but destroying capital —if she waited, she was destroying interest and capital both. Only leave it long enough, and a mere play-bill is worth its weight in gold. That was a wise woman who kept an invitation card of Mrs. Piozzi's.

Keep everything ! say the wise.

And yet this is a counsel of perfection. In London

at any rate we cannot do it, or we die. Given that we must burn, how shall we burn with least offence?

It seems unfair to mingle in a common grave a nine-year-old bill, a love-letter, a legal opinion, and such a pleasing thing as the announcement that there is one more baby in the world. I have felt shocked to hear of a lady who, once a year, carries down her superfluous correspondence in a lump and feeds the kitchen fire with the same. The kitchen fire is fire enslaved and degraded — it is not sacred fire. It roasts the beef, it boils the suet pudding. Letters —even inferior letters—are too good to be used for cookery.

To speculate on the fine food that has fed fire is a favourite form of dreaming with one here and another there. Did it ever eat anything of Shakespeare's? All his letters, no doubt. Many of the plays of Webster it ate—many also by the author of *The City Madam*. But that was the cook's fault. Molière's cook would never have acted thus. She would have been cooked herself first.

Many an autobiography that might have set the world ablaze had it been published, has doubtless gone that way. The fire is a great devourer of Lives. It is incredible how few autobiographies there are! One could count them on one's fingers. The fire alone knows how many were written. I mean, of course, autobiographies of great men. (The little men write theirs fast enough—and wonderfully good reading they are!)

Dante wrote a fragment of his Life; and to this day no one knows what he meant. Perhaps, as he held the opinion that every sentence should have four meanings, this is not to be marvelled at. Goethe wrote his, and wilfully jumbled it up with fiction. Scott tried to write his and broke down altogether.

A little altar might be raised for the destruction of certain letters, with blue flames on it and a sweet smell of incense. There are words that in the burning must leave behind an exquisite perfume—cedar-wood words.

> " With what frankincense and myrrh,
> Burn these precious parts of her ? "

Very life-like is the dying of a letter in fire !

> " Writhing still, as if with grief,
> Went the life from every leaf."

I have seen the characters flash out silver upon black for an instant before they vanished. The corners curl with a kind of magnetism like hair ; the edges shrivel and retire. To a lover of conflagration thick postcards are delightful to burn ; the corners curl different ways.

That most charming of modern French heroines, Mademoiselle Chiffon, was wont to burn her dead flowers. Indeed, it is a heartless thing to throw flowers on a dust-heap. How the fire leaps round as if it loved them, tracing the delicate outline in a thousand sparks, kissing while it consumes ! There would seem to be a secret affinity between flowers and flames. Our fires are made of trees that have known, long ago, blossoms upon their boughs. There must be somewhere a garden of fire. And in that Eden, it may be, the poor heretics of letters flower brightly in flame.

The Drawing-Room

I sometimes wonder how the room I sit in looks to other eyes.

" Do you live in *London* all the year round ? " people say ; and then, even if they are too civil to condole, their eyes take a compassionate expression. Alas, how that good thing, pity, is wasted ! Who would be so lavish of love or of money ? Once—once only I think

—it happened to me to be envied. " You people who live in *London* do not know how glorious it is. You cannot ! " said a British Resident in Foreign Parts, whose drawing-room was a jungle.

To have lived in one place ever since memory began is to have seen that place change as you change yourself ; but more perceptibly. Our own faces and figures in a glass are strange to us as the forms of those with whom we are not acquainted. I do not know after what fashion the little girl who played battledore and shuttlecock here differed from the big girl who came after her, and the woman who now sits in her place. But I know that long ago the drawing-room was much larger than it is now, all the chairs and tables much higher, and the piano unaccountably higher still. It was a vast space of country in those days. I owned a little of it here and there—a dusty cabinet in the backwoods where my story-books lived—and everything underneath the piano. The rest had nothing to do with me. The beautiful brick towers almost as high as myself that I built upon that alien territory were doomed to fall, a few minutes after they were finished. I grieved for them. It seemed to me that they adorned the drawing-room.

In the firelight, of a winter's evening, my possessions expanded. As I danced in and out of the wreaths of white roses on the faded crimson ground of the carpet, I thought those also were mine. And if I had a cold, the sofa belonged to me.

After that came a dreadful time, when I was shut out of the drawing-room almost entirely. An exile feels as I used to feel when I passed the door. Within there was quiet, peace, music, and books to read that were never dull. Without—sums, scales, French verbs, and everything to make existence dreary. Even if I did get in, I was turned out remorselessly when a particular clock struck, and whenever people began to say something I should like to have heard.

By-and-by, when there were parties, I was brought down to sit with a book behind the piano. Thus I made the acquaintance of *King Lear* and was not greatly horrified. Thence I witnessed a love-scene for the first time. My Aunt called me away, afraid lest my too evident sympathy should interrupt it.

A little later on, I came to view the drawing-room in the light of a Theatre. There did I appear, first as the Beast in a black mask, then as the radiant red velvet Prince, wedding his Beauty—I did enact Theseus—I was a wandering Duchess—I was a Puritan in red ancestral boots. The drawing-room was musical with sweet voices then—full of people coming and going. Once I remember that we danced there.

As I sit alone, I wonder who will come when I also have gone.

I should like to think of another child—merrier—not so much afraid of the dark on the stairs outside—and that her mother would play and sing. I should like to think of another girl—as gay, as full of bold ambition and not so shy—acting and dancing where I danced and acted. I hope she will see the greatest man in the world come in, as I saw Robert Browning come through the door one evening, his hat under his arm. I wonder whether she will train the creeper over the balcony to the West and plant geranium and mignonette, and sit there in summer to watch the gold of sunset over the roofs. Bright be her pictures in that shining window, and may she sometimes love a book that I loved !

HILAIRE BELLOC

Our Inheritance

How noble is our inheritance. The more one thinks of it the more suffused with pleasure one's mind becomes ; for the inheritance of a man living in this country is not one of this sort or of that sort, but of all sorts. It is, indeed, a necessary condition for the enjoyment of that inheritance that a man should be free, and we have really so muddled things that very many men in England are not free, for they have either to suffer a gross denial of mere opportunity—I mean they cannot even leave their town for any distance—or they are so persecuted by the insecurity of their lives that they have no room for looking at the world, but if an Englishman is free what an inheritance he has to enjoy !

It is the fashion of great nations to insist upon some part of their inheritance, their military memories, or their letters, or their religion, or some other thing. But in modern Europe, as it seems to me, three or four of the great nations can play upon many such titles to joy as upon an instrument. For a man in Italy, or England, or France, or Spain, if he is weary of the manifold literature of his own country, can turn to its endurance under arms (in which respect, by the way, victory and defeat are of little account), or if he is weary of these military things, or thinks the too continued contemplation of them hurtful to the

State (as it often is, for it goes to the head like wine), he can consider the great minds which his nation has produced, and which give glory to his nation not so much because they are great as because they are national. Then, again, he can consider the land-scapes of his own land, whether peaceably, as do older men, or in a riot of enthusiasm as do all younger men who see England in the midst of exercising their bodies, as it says in the Song of the Man who Bicycled :

> " . . . and her distance and her sea.
> Here is wealth that has no measure,
> All wide England is my treasure,
> Park and Close and private pleasure
> All her hills were made for me."

Then he can poke about the cities, and any one of them might occupy him almost for a lifetime. Hereford, for instance. I know of nothing in Europe like the Norman work of Hereford or Ludlow, where you will perpetually find new things, or Leominster just below, or Ledbury just below that again ; and the inn at each of these three places is called The Feathers.

Then a man may be pleased to consider the re-corded history of this country, and to inform the fields he knows with the past and with the actions of men long dead. In this way he can use a battlefield with no danger of any detestable insolence or vulgar civilian ways, for the interest in a battlefield, if it is closely studied, becomes so keen and hot that it burns away all foolish violence, and you will soon find if you study this sort of terrain closely that you forget on which side your sympathies fail or succeed : an excellent corrective if, as it should be with healthy men, your sympathies too often warp evidence and blind you. On this account also one should always suspect the accuracy of military history when it betrays sneering or crowing, because, in the first place, that is a very unmilitary way of looking at battles, and, in the second place, it argues that the historian has not properly gone into all his details. If he had he would have been much too interested in such questions as the measurement of ranges, or, latterly, the presence and nature of cover to bother about crowing or sneering.

When a man tires of these there is left to him the music of his country, by which I mean the tunes. These he can sing to himself as he goes along, and if ever he tires of that there is the victuals and the drink, which, if he has travelled, he may compare to their advantage over those of any other land. But they must be national. Let him take no pleasure in things cooked in a foreign way. There was a man some time ago, in attempting to discover whose name I have spent too much energy, who wrote a most admirable essay upon cold beef and pickles, remarking that these two elements of English life are retreating as it were into the strongholds where England is still holding out against the dirty cosmopolitan mud which threatens every country to-day. He traced the retreat of cold beef and pickles eastward towards the City from the West End all along Piccadilly and the Strand right into Fleet Street, where, he said, they were keeping their positions manfully. They stand also isolated and besieged in one hundred happy English country towns. . . .

The trouble about writing an article like this is that one wanders about : it is also the pleasure of it. The limits or trammels to an article like this are that, by a recent and very dangerous superstition, the printed truth is punishable at law, and all one's memories of a thousand places upon the Icknield Way, the Stane Street, the Pilgrim's Way, the Rivers Ouse (all three of them), the Cornish Road, the Black Mountain,

Ferry Side, the Three Rivers, all the Pennines, all the Cheviots, all the Cotswolds, all the Mendips, all the Chilterns, all the Malvern Hills, and all the Downs—to speak of but a few—must be memories of praise —by order of the Court. One may not blame : therefore I say nothing of Northwich.

.   .   .   .

Some men say that whereas wealth can be accumulated and left to others when we die, this sort of inheritance can not, and that the great pleasure a man took in his own land and the very many ways in which he found that pleasure and his increase in that pleasure as his life proceeded, all die with him. This you will very often hear deplored. As noble a woman as ever lived in London used to say, speaking of her father (and she also is dead), that all she valued in him died with him, although he had left her a considerable fortune. By which she meant that not only in losing him she had lost a rooted human affection and had suffered what all must suffer, because there is a doom upon us, but that those particular things in which he was particularly favoured had gone away for ever. His power over other languages and over his own language, his vast knowledge of his own county, his acquired courtesy and humour, all mellowed by the world and time, these, she said, were altogether gone. And to us of a younger generation it was her work to lament that we should never know what had once been in England. Among others she vastly admired the first Duke of Wellington, and said that he was tall—which was absurd. Now this noble woman, it seems to me, was in error, for all of us who have loved and enjoyed know not only that we carry something with us elsewhere (as we are bound to believe), but leave also in some manner which I do not clearly perceive a legacy to our own people. We take with us that of which

Peter Wanderwide spoke when he said or rather sang these lines—

> " If all that I have loved and seen
>   Be with me on the Judgment Day,
> I shall be saved the crowd between
>   From Satan and his foul array."

We carry it with us. And though it is not a virtue it is half a virtue, and when we go down in the grave like the character in *Everyman*, there will go down with us, I think, not only Good Deeds, a severe female, but also a merry little hobbling comrade who winks and grins and keeps just behind her so that he shall not be noticed and driven away. This little fellow will also speak for us, I think, and he is the Pleasure we took in this jolly world.

But I say that not only do we carry something with us, but that we leave something also ; and this has been best put, I think, by the poet Ronsard when he was dying, who said, if I have rightly translated him, this—

" Of all those vanities " (he is speaking of the things of this world), " the loveliest and most praiseworthy is glory—fame. No one of my time has been so filled with it as I ; I have lived in it and loved and triumphed in it through time past, and now I leave it to my country to garner and possess it after I shall die. So do I go away from my own place as satiated with the glory of this world as I am hungry and all longing for that of God."

That is very good. It would be very difficult to put it better, and if you complain that here Ronsard was only talking of fame or glory, why, I can tell you that the pleasure one takes in one's country is of the same stuff as fame. So true is this that the two commonly go together, and that those become most glorious who have most enjoyed their own land.

EDWARD THOMAS

Broken Memories

" Mr. ——, the well-known merchant, is building a fine
house, half a mile from the —— Road.   Close upon two
acres of woodland have been felled, where, by the way,
the largest and juiciest blackberries I know used to be
found."—*London Local Newspaper.*

AND in this way many suburbans have seen the paradise of their boyhood effaced.   The building rises
during some long farewell, and steals away a fraction
of the very sky in which once we beheld Orion sink
down like a falling sword into the west and its line of
battlemented woods.   Only here and there a coppice
will survive, blockaded by houses a-row.   Sometimes
a well-beloved pleasaunce is left almost as it was ; the
trees are the same ; the voices are the same ; a silence
is there still ; but there is a caret somewhere—in ourselves or in the place.   In childhood we went there as
often as our legs could bear us so far ; oftener yet in
youth ; but less and less with time.   Then, perhaps,
we travel—anyway we live feverishly and variously ;
and only think of the old places when the fire is tran-
quil and lights are out, and " each into himself de-
scends," or when we meet one who was once a friend,
or when we lay open a forgotten drawer.   A very
slender chain only binds us to the gods of forest and
field—but binds us nevertheless.   Then we take the
old walk, it may be, in a walking suit of the best ;
fearful of mire · carrying a field-glass too ; and smok-

ing the pipe that used to seem an insult so intolerable in the great woods. We take the old walk, and it seems shorter than before, a walk not formidable at all, as it was in the years when the end used to find us testy with fatigue and overpowered by tumultuous impressions ; when we ourselves thought the sea itself could not be far, and the names of village and hill we visited were unknown.

A railway bisects the common we cross. Everything is haggard and stale ; the horizon is gone ; and the spirit chafes and suffocates for lack of it. (But the gorse is in flower still.) Then the feet weary on gravel paths downhill. On either side are fields, edged by flaccid suburban grass, with an odour as of tombs—as though nothing fair could blossom in a soil that must be the sepulchre of many divinities. And again the pathway is dogged by houses, interrupting the fields. The former sanity and amenity of air is gone. We can no longer shorten the way to the next houses by a path from the willowy river-side over fields, for the willows are down, the fields heavily burdened with streets. Another length of mean houses, neither urban nor rustic, but both, where I remember the wretched children's discordant admiration of the abounding gold hair of a passer-by ; and soon the bridge over a railway gives a view across plantations of cabbage, etc. But the view is comforting—there is an horizon ! There is an horizon barred with poplar trees to the south ; the streets are behind, in the north. The horizon is dear to us yet, as the possible home of the unknown and the greatly desired, as the apparent birthplace and tomb of setting and rising suns ; from under it the clouds mount, and under it again they return after crossing the sky. A mystery is about it as when we were children playing upon a broad, treeless common, and actually long continued running in pursuit of the horizon.

After three miles in all we leave the turnpike, to

follow a new but grassy road out among the fields, under lines of acacia and poplar and horse-chestnut last. Once more the ploughland shows us the twinkling flight of pewits; the well, and the quaking water uplifted in a shining band where it touches the stones; the voices of sparrows while the trees are dripping in the dawn; and overhead the pompous mobilization of cloud armadas, so imposing in a country where they tilt against ebony boughs. . . . In a thicket some gipsies have encamped, and two of them—superb youths, with favours of raven hair blowing across the dusky roses of their cheeks—have jumped from their labour to hear the postman reading their letters. Several pipe-sucking bird-catchers are at watch over an expanse of nets. We cross a ploughland half within the sovereignty of the forest shadow. Here is the wood!

The big wood we called it. So well we knew it, and for so many years—wandered here with weeping like Imogen's, and with laughter like Yorick's laughter—that when past years bulk into the likeness of a forest through which the memory takes its pleasure at eventide,

> " Or in clear dream or solemn vision,"

it is really this wood that we see, under a halcyon sky.

It covered two acres in the midst of ploughland; but we thought of it as enormous, because in it we often lost one another; it had such diversity; it made so genuine a solitude. The straight oaks rising branchless for many feet expanded and then united boughs in a firmament of leaves. It seemed far enough from London for feelings of security. But even of that our thoughts have changed; for the houses are fearfully close—a recollection of them lingers in the heart of the wood; and perhaps they will devour it also. . . . Who shall measure the sorrow of him that hath set his heart upon that which the world hath power to destroy and hath destroyed ? Even to-day the circuit of a cemetery is cutting into the field where we gathered buttercups before the dignity of knickerbockers. . . . And here was a solitude. We cannot summon up any thought or reverie which had not in this wood its nativity. 'Tis we have changed ! And if we could paint, and wished to make a picture of our youth with its seriousness and its folly, we should paint in this wood, instead of in a hostel-yard, another Don Quixote watching his armour all night after the false accolade.

The dark earth itself was pleasant to handle—earth one might wish to be buried in—and had the healthy and special quality of wild earth : upon it you could rest deliciously. (Compare the artificial soil of a London common with it !) Out of this rose up trees that preserved their wild attitudes. The age-fallen or tempest-uprooted oak tree lay where it dropped, or hung balanced in the boughs of others. Tenderest bramble spray or feeler of honeysuckle bridged those gaps in the underwood that served as paths. And the winds were husbandmen, reapers and sowers thereof. Though, indeed, the trees were ordered with an incongruous juxtaposition of birch and oak and elm, it seemed to us a fragment of the primæval forest left by a possible good fortune at the city verge. But it was more than this. With its lofty roof and the mysterious flashes of light in the foliaged clerestory, with its shapely boles in cluster and colonnade, and the glimpses of bright white sky that came and went among the leaves, the forest had a real likeness to a temple. Shelley's " Ode to the West Wind " and passages of Adonais were the *ediscenda* of our devotions.

Here we saw the grim jewellery of winter on fallen leaf and bow of grass ; gold and purple colouring inseparable from the snow upon boughs overhead ;

the hills far away sombre and yet white with snow ;
and on the last of the icy mornings, the sward beaming
with melted frost, and the frost only persisting on the
ample shadows with which the trees stamp the grass.
Here we saw the coming of Spring, when the liquid
orbed leaves of toad-flax crept out of a barren stone.
Full of joy we watched here the " sweet and twenty "
of perfect Summer, when the matin shadows were
once deleted, and the dew-globes evaporated from
the harebell among the fern, or twinkled as they fell
silently underfoot.   But the favourite of memory is
a certain flower-shadowing tree whose branches had
been earthward bent by the swinging of boyish generations.   Foliage and shadow muffled the sight, and
seated there in profound emerald moss, the utmost
you achieved was to find a name for each of the little
thicket flowers.   If you raised your head you would
have seen in a tumultuous spasm of sunshine—say at
mid March—the blue smoke upcoiling between the
boughs of overhanging trees far off and dissipated in
the dashing air ; the trees shining in their leaflessness
like amber and dark agate ; above that the woodland
seared in black upon the heated horizon blue ;—but
you never raised your head.   For hours you could
here have peace, among the shadows embroidered
with flowers of the colour of gold.   All which tantalizes
—sun and clouds and for ever inaccessible horizon—
was locked out ; only (like a golden bar across a
gloomy coat of arms) one sunbeam across the brown
wood ; thrushes and blackbirds warbled unseen. The
soul—this made a cage bird of it. The eagle's apotheo-
sis in the fires of the sun was envied not. What a subtle
diversity of needled herbs and grass there is in the
plainest field carpet ! all miniature after close crop-
ping of rabbit and sheep ; auriferous dandelion,
plumed self-heal, dainty trefoil, plantain, delicate
feathered grasses, starry blossomed heather, illuminations of tormentil, unsearchable moss forests, and there

jewelled insects, rosy centaury ; nearly all in flower together, and the whole not deep enough to hide a field-mouse.

A dim solitude thus circumscribed liked us hugely. We loved not the insolent and importunate splendours of perfect light. Cobwebs and wholesome dust—we needed some of both in the corners of our minds. They mature the wine of the spirit perhaps. We would always have had, as it were, a topmost and nearly inaccessible file of tomes, which we never read, but often planned to read—records peradventure of unvictorious alchymist and astrologer. Thither a sunbeam never penetrated and unmasked. The savour of paraffin and brick-dust should never cling about it. Unfortunate (we thought) is he who has no dusty and never-explored recesses in his mind !

ROBERT LYND

The Darkness

IT was common enough during the first year of the war to meet people who took an æsthetic pleasure in the darkness of the streets at night. It gave them *un nouveau frisson*. They said that never had London been so beautiful. It was hardly a gracious thing to say about London. And it was not entirely true. The hill of Piccadilly has always been beautiful, with its lamps suspended above it like strange fruits. The Thames between Westminster Bridge and Blackfriars has always been beautiful at night, pouring its brown waters along in a dusk of light and shadow. And have we not always had Hyde Park like a little dark forest full of lamps, with the gold of the lamps shaken into long Chinese alphabets in the windy waters of the Serpentine ? There was Chelsea, too. Surely, even before the war, Chelsea by night lay in darkness like a town forgotten and derelict in the snug gloom of an earlier century. And, if Chelsea was pitchy, St. George's-in-the-East and London of the docks were pitchier. There we seemed already to be living underground. The very lamps, yellow as a hag's skin with snuff in every wrinkle, seemed scarcely to give enough light to enable one to see the world of rags and blackness which one was visiting like a stranger from another planet. One finds it so difficult to conjure up the appearance of London in the time before the war that one may be exaggerating. But, so far as one can

remember, night in London was even then something
of an enchantress and London the land of an enchantress. Her palace lights, her dungeon darkness,
her snoring suburbs tucked away into bed after a sur-
feit of the piano and the gramophone—here, even in
days of peace, was an infinite variety of spectacle.
Not that I will pretend that the suburbs were ever
beautiful. They are more depressing than a heap of
old tins, than a field of bricks, than slob-lands, than
vineyards in early summer. They are more commonplace than the misuse of the word " phenomenal " or
the jargon of house-agents. They do not possess
enough character even to be called ugly. They are
the expression in brick of the sin of the Laodiceans.
Neither the light of peace nor the Tartarus of war
can awaken them out of their bad prose. One thinks
of them as the commodious slave-quarters of modern
civilization. The human race has yet to learn, or to
re-learn, how to build suburbs. It is a proof of our
immorality that we cannot do so. Well, the darkness
has at least hidden the face of the suburbs. It has
changed long rows of houses into little cottages, and
monotonous avenues into country lanes down which
cautious figures make their way with torches. Sometimes in these circumstances, the dullest street becomes like a parade of will-o'-the-wisps. The post-
girl alone, with her larger lamp, is impressive as a
motor-car or a policeman. She steps with the self-
assurance of an institution past the images of lost
souls looking for Paradise by candlelight. . . .

Certainly, the first searchlight that waved above
London like a sword was wonderful. That made the
darkness—and Charing Cross—beautiful. The lovers
of darkness were right when they praised searchlights.
Probably the first of them was but a tiny affair compared to those that now lie thick as post-offices
between the hills of north and south London ; but it
impressed the imagination as an adventurer among

the stars. One would not have been unduly surprised if one had caught sight of the prince of the powers of the air making his way on black wings from star to star at the end of its long beam. Later on, London sent forth a hundred such lights. She spent her evenings like a mathematician drawing weird geometrical figures on the darkness. She became the greatest of the Futurists, all cubes and angles. Sometimes she seemed like a crab lying on its back and waving a multitude of inevitable pincers. Sometimes she seemed to be fishing in the sky with an immense dragnet of light. Sometimes, on misty-moisty nights, the searchlights lit up the sluggish clouds with smudges of gold. It was like a decoration of water-lilies on long stems of light. On nights on which a Zeppelin raid was in progress one has seen the distant sky filled, as it were, with lilies, east and west, north and south. And, for many people, the Zeppelins themselves seemed to have beautified the night. For my part, I confess I cannot regard the Zeppelin without prejudice as a spectacle. That it is beautiful as a silver fish, as the lights play on it, I will not deny. Nor can one remain unmoved by the sight as shells burst about it with little sputters, like fireworks on a wet night. But, even as a pyrotechnic display, the Zeppelin raid has, in my opinion, been overestimated. They could do better at the Crystal Palace. As soon as the first novelty of the Zeppelins had worn off, it was their beastliness rather than their beauty that impressed itself upon those with the most persistent passion for sight-seeing. Even the sight of a Zeppelin in flames, awe-inspiring though it was, soon ceased to be a novelty calling for superlatives. All the same, London of the searchlights and the Zeppelins will not be forgotten in sixty years. Men and women now living will relate to their grandchildren how they saw a ship in the sky in a tangle of gold lights, and how the ship was then swallowed up in darkness, and how, after a space of darkness and echoes, the sky suddenly purpled into a false dawn and opened into a rose of light. Then, hung in the air for a moment, was a little ball of flame, and then the darkness again, and only a broken rope of gold hurriedly dropped down the sky to announce the ultimate horror of disaster. Those who had a nearer view of the affair will have their own variant of the story. They, too, will tell how the sky was suddenly flooded with monstrous tides of light at midnight, and how the wonders of morning and sunset were mingled, and how the sunset began to move towards them with its red eye, with its red mouth, a vast furnace-ship, an enemy of the world, increasing, lengthening, a doom impending, till once more darkness and foolish cheers, and laughter and anecdotes in the streets. Assuredly, the darkness of London has had its interesting moments. . . .

One has to admit the attractions even of the common darkness of the streets. Perhaps it has become, from an æsthetic point of view, excessive in recent months, and, except on moonlight nights, we have too much the air of shadowy creatures of the Brocken as we make our way about in the dimness. The tram that used to sail along like a ship with all its lights burning was certainly a prettier thing to see than the dismal bus of these days, packed like a doss-house, charging into obscurity. A long line of taxicabs can still give a street in a busy hour the appearance of a stream of stars, and on a wet evening even a procession of vans with their red lights reflected in the pavement can impart to the commonest road the magic of a Venetian canal. But the darkness is by no means so beautiful now as it was when a few windows were still left lighted. At the time of the first lighting regulations, we were given a subdued light instead of a glare. Buildings with every feature a misunderstanding revealed themselves as impressive masses; illuminated advertisements disappeared; and we could still see to read the evening paper in a bus, so that we were rather gratified, or at least disinclined to grumble. Now, however, we have reached the stage of real darkness. To go out in it is, as I heard a servant remark, like going into the coal-hole without a candle. There are parts of the town in which even the soberest man may walk into a tree or a lamp-post, and there is almost no part of the town in which during the dark of the moon a man may not fall down a flight of stone steps—and will not, if he does not carry an electric torch. Perhaps the best compensation Londoners have been given for the darkness is the pleasing variety of the means by which the lights have been dimmed in different neighbourhoods. In some suburbs the lamps look as though they had been dirtied like a slut's face. Elsewhere they wear masks pierced with holes, and are terrible and black like inquisitors or mediæval executioners. Some of them are blue, some green, some brown, some flamingo-coloured. London, that lawless city, was never more admirably lawless than in this. Light falls from many of them like the veils that little children wear in Catholic countries on taking their first communion. From others it falls like the garment of a ghost. Other lights give the effect of a row of Chinese lanterns hung high above a high street. But there is no sense of merriment amid all these fantastic odds and ends of lights. The light regulations have manifestly muted the life of London. Even the Australian and Canadian soldiers who pace so determinedly up and down the Strand and hang in groups round every corner, have an elfin unsubstantial appearance among the shadows. Men not in khaki look black as Hamlets. Girls of the plainest are mysteries till one hears their voices. The porches of theatres are filled with a blue mystic light that would make one speak in whispers. Night certainly falls on London like a blanket. Perhaps it is mostly illusion. There is, as they say, all the fun of the fair going on for those who are young and giddy of heart, and London is not without laughter and loud voices and reeling figures. But the effect is, undoubtedly, depressing. Public-houses, darkened like prisons, no longer invite the mob with bright and vulgar windows. Cinematograph theatres are as gloomy-fronted as though over their doors they bore the motto : " Abandon hope, all ye who enter here." Rather than venture into such a wilderness of joylessness, many people prefer to sit at home and play tiddleywinks. Or argue. How they argue !

Luckily, in the beginning, there were created, along with the earth, a sun and a moon, and neither policeman nor magistrate nor any other creature has any power over them of regulation or control. It is the moon that makes London by night beautiful in war-time. It is the moon that makes the north side of Trafalgar Square white with romance like a Moorish city, and makes the South Kensington Museum itself appear as though it had been built to music. London under the moon is a city of wonder, a city of fair streets and fair citizens. Under the moon the arc-lamps in their cowls no longer affect us like sentinel killjoys. They seem feeble and insignificant as dying torches when the moonlight performs her miracles and exalts this city of mean dwellings into a beauty equal to that of the restless sea.

GILBERT K. CHESTERTON

A Defence of Penny Dreadfuls

One of the strangest examples of the degree to which ordinary life is undervalued is the example of popular literature, the vast mass of which we contentedly describe as vulgar. The boy's novelette may be ignorant in a literary sense, which is only like saying that a modern novel is ignorant in the chemical sense, or the economic sense, or the astronomical sense ; but it is not vulgar intrinsically—it is the actual centre of a million flaming imaginations.

In former centuries the educated class ignored the ruck of vulgar literature. They ignored, and therefore did not, properly speaking, despise it. Simple ignorance and indifference does not inflate the character with pride. A man does not walk down the street giving a haughty twirl to his moustaches at the thought of his superiority to some variety of deep-sea fishes. The old scholars left the whole under-world of popular compositions in a similar darkness.

To-day, however, we have reversed this principle. We do despise vulgar compositions, and we do not ignore them. We are in some danger of becoming petty in our study of pettiness ; there is a terrible Circean law in the background that if the soul stoops too ostentatiously to examine anything it never gets up again. There is no class of vulgar publications about which there is, to my mind, more utterly ridiculous exaggeration and misconception than the current boys' literature of the lowest stratum. This class of composition has presumably always existed, and must exist. It has no more claim to be good literature than the daily conversation of its readers to be fine oratory, or the lodging-houses and tenements they inhabit to be sublime architecture. But people must have conversation, they must have houses, and they must have stories. The simple need for some kind of ideal world in which fictitious persons play an unhampered part is infinitely deeper and older than the rules of good art, and much more important. Every one of us in childhood has constructed such an invisible *dramatis personæ*, but it never occurred to our nurses to correct the composition by careful comparison with Balzac. In the East the professional story-teller goes from village to village with a small carpet; and I wish sincerely that any one had the moral courage to spread that carpet and sit on it in Ludgate Circus. But it is not probable that all the tales of the carpet-bearer are little gems of original artistic workmanship. Literature and fiction are two entirely different things. Literature is a luxury; fiction is a necessity. A work of art can hardly be too short, for its climax is its merit. A story can never be too long, for its conclusion is merely to be deplored, like the last halfpenny or the last pipelight. And so, while the increase of the artistic conscience tends in more ambitious works to brevity and impressionism, voluminous industry still marks the producer of the true romantic trash. There was no end to the ballads of Robin Hood; there is no end to the volumes about Dick Deadshot and the Avenging Nine. These two heroes are deliberately conceived as immortal.

But instead of basing all discussion of the problem upon the common-sense recognition of this fact—that the youth of the lower orders always has had and always must have formless and endless romantic reading of some kind, and then going on to make provision for its wholesomeness—we begin, generally speaking, by fantastic abuse of this reading as a whole and indignant surprise that the errand-boys under discussion do not read *The Egoist* and *The Master Builder*. It is the custom, particularly among magistrates, to attribute half the crimes of the Metropolis to cheap novelettes. If some grimy urchin runs away with an apple, the magistrate shrewdly points out that the child's knowledge that apples appease hunger is traceable to some curious literary researches. The boys themselves, when penitent, frequently accuse the novelettes with great bitterness, which is only to be expected from young people possessed of no little native humour. If I had forged a will, and could obtain sympathy by tracing the incident to the influence of Mr. George Moore's novels, I should find the greatest entertainment in the diversion. At any rate, it is firmly fixed in the minds of most people that gutter-boys, unlike everybody else in the community, find their principal motives for conduct in printed books.

Now it is quite clear that this objection, the objection brought by magistrates, has nothing to do with literary merit. Bad story writing is not a crime. Mr. Hall Caine walks the streets openly, and cannot be put in prison for an anticlimax. The objection rests upon the theory that the tone of the mass of boys' novelettes is criminal and degraded, appealing to low cupidity and low cruelty. This is the magisterial theory, and this is rubbish.

So far as I have seen them, in connection with the dirtiest bookstalls in the poorest districts, the facts are simply these : The whole bewildering mass of vulgar juvenile literature is concerned with adventures, rambling, disconnected, and endless. It does not express any passion of any sort, for there is no human character of any sort. It runs eternally in certain grooves of local and historical type : the mediæval knight, the eighteenth-century duellist, and the modern cowboy recur with the same stiff simplicity as the conventional human figures in an Oriental pattern.   I can quite as easily imagine a human being kindling wild appetites by the contemplation of his Turkey carpet as by such dehumanized and naked narrative as this.

Among these stories there are a certain number which deal sympathetically with the adventures of robbers, outlaws, and pirates, which present in a dignified and romantic light thieves and murderers like Dick Turpin and Claude Duval.   That is to say, they do precisely the same thing as Scott's *Ivanhoe*, Scott's *Rob Roy*, Scott's *Lady of the Lake*, Byron's *Corsair*, Wordsworth's *Rob Roy's Grave*, Stevenson's *Macaire*, Mr. Max Pemberton's *Iron Pirate*, and a thousand more works distributed systematically as prizes and Christmas presents.   Nobody imagines that an admiration of Locksley in *Ivanhoe* will lead a boy to shoot Japanese arrows at the deer in Richmond Park ; no one thinks that the incautious opening of Wordsworth at the poem on Rob Roy will set him up for life as a blackmailer.   In the case of our own class, we recognize that this wild life is contemplated with pleasure by the young, not because it is like their own life, but because it is different from it.   It might at least cross our minds that, for whatever other reason the errand-boy reads *The Red Revenge*, it really is not because he is dripping with the gore of his own friends and relatives.

In this matter, as in all such matters, we lose our bearings entirely by speaking of the " lower classes " when we mean humanity minus ourselves.   This trivial romantic literature is not especially plebeian : it is simply human.   The philanthropist can never forget classes and callings.   He says, with a modest swagger, " I have invited twenty-five factory hands to tea." If he said, " I have invited twenty-five chartered accountants to tea," every one would see the humour of so simple a classification.   But this is what we have done with this lumberland of foolish writing : we have probed, as if it were some monstrous new disease, what is, in fact, nothing but the foolish and valiant heart of man. Ordinary men will always be sentimentalists : for a sentimentalist is simply a man who has feelings and does not trouble to invent a new way of expressing them. These common and current publications have nothing essentially evil about them. They express the sanguine and heroic truisms on which civilization is built ; for it is clear that unless civilization is built on truisms, it is not built at all. Clearly, there could be no safety for a society in which the remark by the Chief Justice that murder was wrong was regarded as an original and dazzling epigram.

If the authors and publishers of *Dick Deadshot*, and such remarkable works, were suddenly to make a raid upon the educated class, were to take down the names of every man, however distinguished, who was caught at a University Extension Lecture, were to confiscate all our novels and warn us all to correct our lives, we should be seriously annoyed. Yet they have far more right to do so than we ; for they, with all their idiotcy, are normal and we are abnormal. It is the modern literature of the educated, not of the uneducated, which is avowedly and aggressively criminal. Books recommending profligacy and pessimism, at which the high-souled errand-boy would shudder, lie upon all our drawing-room tables. If the dirtiest old owner of the dirtiest old bookstall in Whitechapel dared to display works really recommending polygamy or suicide, his stock would be seized by the police. These things are our luxuries. And with a hypocrisy so ludicrous as to be almost unparalleled in history, we rate the gutter-boys for their immorality at the very time that we are discussing (with equivocal German professors) whether morality is valid at all. At the very instant that we curse the Penny Dreadful for encouraging thefts upon property, we canvass the proposition that all property is theft. At the very instant we accuse it (quite unjustly) of lubricity and indecency, we are cheerfully reading philosophies which glory in lubricity and indecency. At the very instant that we charge it with encouraging the young to destroy life, we are placidly discussing whether life is worth preserving.

But it is we who are the morbid exceptions ; it is we who are the criminal class. This should be our great comfort. The vast mass of humanity, with their vast mass of idle books and idle words, have never doubted and never will doubt that courage is splendid, that fidelity is noble, that distressed ladies should be rescued, and vanquished enemies spared. There are a large number of cultivated persons who doubt these maxims of daily life, just as there are a large number of persons who believe they are the Prince of Wales ; and I am told that both classes of people are entertaining conversationalists. But the average man or boy writes daily in these great gaudy diaries of his soul, which we call Penny Dreadfuls, a plainer and better gospel than any of those iridescent ethical paradoxes that the fashionable change as often as their bonnets. It may be a very limited aim in morality to shoot a " many-faced and fickle traitor," but at least it is a better aim than to be a many-faced and fickle traitor, which is a simple summary of a good many modern systems from Mr. d'Annunzio's downwards. So long as the coarse and thin texture of mere current popular romance is not touched by a paltry culture it will never be vitally immoral. It is always on the side of life. The poor—the slaves who really stoop under the burden of life—have often been mad, scatterbrained, and cruel, but never hopeless. That is a class privilege, like cigars. Their drivelling literature will always be a " blood and thunder " literature, as simple as the thunder of heaven and the blood of men.

PRINTED IN GREAT BRITAIN AT
THE PRESS OF THE PUBLISHERS